The
John Hannam
Showbiz Interviews

The
John Hannam
Showbiz Interviews

The revealing stories behind
John's memorable interviews with the stars
of stage and screen past and present

This book is dedicated to
Keith Newbery and Roberta Crismass

Personal thanks to those who have helped in various ways
with the publication of this book.

Ena and Roy Hannam, my late parents, who gave me so much
encouragement, Sean and Caroline for their continued support,
Brian Greening, Adrian Nigh, Mike Lambert, Diane and Peter Eames,
Celia and John Vosper, Vic Farrow, Isle of Wight Radio, the artists,
their agents and managements, theatre press officers, tour company
managers, holiday centre staff, so many friendly faces in theatres and
recording studios, newspaper and magazine editors, press photographers
and members of the public for interview opportunities and suggestions.

Keith Newbery with John

Roberta (Bertie) Crismass and John

First published 2017 by John Hannam. Copyright © John Hannam

Book design by Mike Lambert, Freshwater, Isle of Wight PO40 9PP

Printed by Short Run Press Limited
25 Bittern Road, Sowton Industrial Estate, Exeter, Devon EX2 7LW

ISBN 978-0-9504126-5-8

ALSO AVAILABLE is John Hannam's book recalling his
interviews with pop stars from the '50s, '60s and '70s.
Some gave him a rough time, others were full of their
own importance and some took him by surprise!

Contents

John Hannam

John with Des O'Connor

BACK IN 1974 when John began interviewing famous people, as a freelance showbiz journalist and broadcaster, he made a policy that he would only undertake in-person interviews. Over the years this may have lost him a few huge names but he has bravely stuck to his principals. This makes him somewhat unique in a business where down-the-line interviews are now quite often the preferred choice of artists and PR companies. For John, actually meeting his guests is of paramount importance and he's never been looking for a quick ten minutes into a music-based radio show. In his many years as a showbusiness feature writer he has always applied the same rule.

John thrives on doing hours of research for many interviews and has a friendly technique, which has been praised by numerous star names over the past 40 years. Many have gone out of their way to congratulate him. John prides himself on being a member of the old school of chat show hosts. He's had no desire to be the star of the show or to use his guests as pure fodder for cheap laughs. Private lives have never been on his agenda and his interviewees have always trusted him profusely. So much so, that on occasions, they have just opened up to reveal unexpected stories.

John has gained such a high reputation within the industry and Radio 2 have used around 20 of his archive recordings for their national radio shows. His archive is rated as one of the best in the British Isles. With over 4000 interviews to his name, it's easy to see why. Now the Hannam Archive podcasts are listened to all around the world.

This book features the stories behind nearly 100 of these interviews and he reveals memorable moments with Bruce Forsyth, John Mills, Charlton Heston, Benny Hill, Donald Pleasence, Sheridan Smith, Edward Windsor and many others.

How times have changed for John and his ilk. In his early days there were still opportunities just to turn up at a gig and get interviews with major stars. There were no PR people timing the interviews or over-protective agents and managements. He's also had proof, in more recent years, that requests for interviews are not always passed on to the artists.

Luckily, over 40 years, John has made many friends in the business and has built up a reputation of being fully trustworthy and a perfect professional. Thankfully, so many have stayed loyal to him. Company managers and press officers have always gone out of their way to assist him. John is so grateful to all of those in the business who continue to help him.

John's new and archive interviews can be heard all over the world on regular new online podcasts. Links can be obtained from John's website www.johnhannam.com plus the Isle of Wight Radio website, iTunes and Audioboom.

Foreword by Jimmy Tarbuck

DURING MY 60 YEARS in showbusiness, I have been interviewed by many people and you get asked to say a few words or sometimes for your opinions. I have been at ease with some and others you just don't speak to. With John, you know he will interview you and tell it as it is. That's why so many colleagues of mine enjoy having an interview with the Isle of Wight King.

He did shock me the first time I met him in 1979 when he said to me 'I've got a little Dictaphone' – so I told him you can't have everything mate.

If you look at a list of his interviews I honestly don't think there is anybody from the A division of showbusiness who he hasn't interviewed, spoken to, written about and, most of all, become friends with. He's a lucky man because he lives in that little paradise called the Isle of Wight, where we all enjoy going to perform or sometimes just visiting for a little break.

On my visits I got to know John very well, especially at our after show fish and chip party nights at Sandown Pavilion, which unfortunately had a serious fire whilst I was there in 1989 – but not because of the fish and chip nights – or John's little Dictaphone!

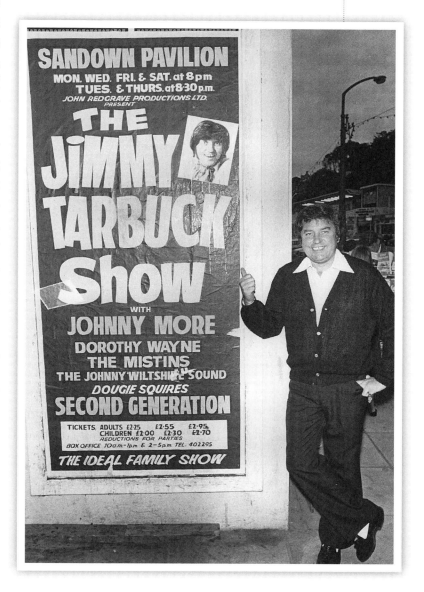

He's a walking encyclopedia of showbiz and what I like about him is that he's very fond of my side of the business, which these days is called variety. You say that to some journalists and they don't know what you're talking about, but John does.

You'll enjoy the book and I'm sure on several pages there will be your own personal favourites. So enjoy, keep well and as John has said to me many times – there's no business like showbusiness.

**Best Wishes,
Jimmy Tarbuck**

Introduction

John Hannam

WHEN I LOOK BACK on my life, I consider I was born at the perfect time to see real stars perform, whether on stage or in some memorable black and white movies in numerous local cinemas. My parents, Roy, who was a linotype operator at the *Isle of Wight County Press*, and Ena, a housewife, somehow managed to bring up my sister and I with very little money to spare. There were no foreign holidays – or even holidays, come to that. We had days out and the highlight for me was always our visits to the Theatre Royal, Portsmouth, to see the dying days of variety.

John's Mum and Dad

There was the excitement of the ferry crossing from Ryde to Portsmouth and the chance to queue at the stage door to collect autographs and photographs of both the stars and the support acts. I can remember Tony Brent being my first singing idol and the delight of obtaining his autograph. Others on those shows included a very young Harry Secombe, Brian Reece, who was radio's PC 49, the Skyliners, Barry Took and Michael Bentine. Occasionally we went to the nearby Empire Theatre, which was a little more downmarket. I did see Frankie Vaughan there in just his third week in showbiz. I can always remember visits to the summer shows at the South Parade Pier, Southsea, to see stars like Arthur English and 'Monsieur' Eddie Gray. Before the shows you could have tea in the ballroom and listen to star organists, including Reginald Porter-Brown.

In my teenage years there were Sunday Celebrity Concerts at Sandown Pavilion and Shanklin Theatre. It was the same show at both theatres, with the top of the bill closing the first half at Shanklin and then taking the taxi ride, with other acts, to Sandown to close the show there. Some big names came. I saw Dick Emery, Joan Regan, The Springfields, Jon Pertwee, Adam Faith, Terry Scott and Hugh Lloyd and Craig Douglas.

I loved resident summer shows and travelled to many across southern England. Locally, some of the comedians who came included Cyril Fletcher, Bobby Dennis, Felix Bowness, Frankie Holmes, Bill Pertwee and Billy Burden. Later in the halcyon days of Sandown Pavilion came Jimmy Tarbuck, Frankie Howerd, Norman Wisdom, Ted Rogers, Cilla Black, Little and Large, Larry Grayson and Matt Monro.

I loved reading *The Stage*, then more of a light entertainment bible, to see who was playing where. Later I went on to write features and reviews for them. My enthusiasm and love for showbusiness has never wavered since those days. Interviewing over 4000 people has been such a joy and these include some of my earliest screen idols like Charlton Heston, Jack Warner, Richard Todd, Donald Pleasence, John Mills and Liz Fraser.

John Hannam

Jon Pertwee

Brian Reece

CHAPTER 1

Alan Rickman

I USED TO WATCH Alan Rickman in movies and top television series and marvelled at his incredible acting talents. I never thought I would ever meet him. It actually happened on April 26, 2008, in Newport, on the Isle of Wight. Ironically, neither of us would have wanted to be there. It was at the Minster Church for the Thanksgiving Service for the life of Anthony Minghella, a man we both had so much admiration for. His sudden death had shocked movie lovers all around the world. Anthony was such a great admirer of Alan's work and gave him the chance to star in his first-ever movie, *Truly Madly Deeply*. I'd known Anthony since his school days when his parents ran a cafe and made gorgeous ice creams.

After the service, we went to the nearby Quay Arts Centre, where both famous and local friends of Anthony's mingled together. I was hesitant to go and speak to Alan but was encouraged to do so by one of Anthony's life-long pals, Graeme du Fresne. They were mates on the Isle of Wight and played in the same local pop group. Graeme, also a composer and actor, who played a ghost in *Truly Madly Deeply*, knew Alan and had a word on my behalf. We briefly met and I asked him if I could interview him at some stage and dedicate it to the memory of Anthony. He gave me his agent's details and a few weeks later we met up on a Saturday morning in the Ellington Lodge at the Concorde, Eastleigh. At that time he was involved with a musical dance show in Eastleigh, which actually included Anthony's recorded voice.

I asked Alan for his own reflections of his good friend.

"With Anthony it was very much his human qualities that everyone remembers. It was always a human interaction between him and his actors. On *Truly Madly Deeply* he was wise enough to include many actors he had worked with in the theatre.

"As the writer of the movie he wrote the most speakable dialogue and when you read it in the script, you wanted to say it."

About 20 minutes into our interview we thought a jet had landed at the nearby Southampton Airport, but Alan looked outside to see 50 guys on motorbikes. We had to have a temporary break. I teased him a wee bit and asked him if he'd ever been a biker. I was not surprised to find out that he hadn't.

When Alan directed his first movie, *The Winter Guest*, Anthony had invited him to their editing suite in America to see them working on *The English Patient*. He was so grateful for this and to be allowed to voice his own thoughts.

In the early days he never really expected to be a movie star or even appear in a film like *Die Hard*, where he became world famous as Hans Gruber.

"It was a classic of its type and every black character in it was a positive role model. It had real wit and visual flair and was a simple story terribly well told."

Was it true he only got the role because he was cheap? He grinned and didn't deny it. His life certainly changed, anyway.

Colonel Brandon in *Pride And Prejudice* was such a beautiful contrast and everyone had such sympathy for his character - and there was a happy ending with a double wedding. He also appeared in *Robin Hood: Prince Of Thieves*, *Sweeney Todd* and the Harry Potter movies.

Alan had come a long way from delivering Nigel Hawthorne's shirts to his dressing room in his spare time job, while at RADA.

It was another shock and a great loss to the movie industry when Alan died in early 2016.

CHAPTER 2

Val Doonican

WHEN YOU ARE an interviewer, patience is a great virtue. Back in the '70s I waited for five hours to interview Joe Loss and he then gave me five minutes. It took me fully 18 years to finally chat to Gene Pitney. I had given up all hope of Val Doonican until a mutual friend spoke up on my behalf. The genial Irishman then gave me his first press interview for many years – and I owed it all to a great comedian called Peter Hudson.

Apparently, on the way home from a Sunday concert at Sandown Pavilion, Peter, his support act, asked Val if he had been interviewed by me. In essence he hadn't, as his management had again turned me down. Peter put a good word in for me and in 1985 I finally caught up with Val and I think I'm safe to say we both enjoyed the experience.

The proof was in the fact that Val always chatted to me on his future visits. In 1989, we had taken a weeks holiday in Yorkshire and had planned to come back on the Sunday, as I was due to interview Val backstage at Sandown Pavilion, before his show. At the Southampton ferry terminal, we just caught the final few words of a Radio Solent news bulletin which indicated a local theatre had been severely damaged by fire. We had missed the name of the theatre but, for some reason, I feared the worst – and so it proved. It was Sandown Pavilion and the concert had been cancelled.

When I'd first met Val in 1985 he'd enjoyed 14 hit singles and his BBC TV series had been watched by 10 million viewers – but he had no current recording contract. Mind you, that year it would have been hard to imagine Val sandwiched between Madonna, Tears For Fears and Wham in the pop charts.

With 23 television series under his belt Val was not overly concerned. During his 40 years in showbiz he had achieved so much. His enthusiasm and excitement for showbusiness had never changed. Back home in Waterford, he'd hitched a 100 miles to buy his first guitar.

He told me: "I'm so sad when I meet people who are cynical about our business. It's the best job in the world. You can earn money if you succeed and be treated so

well everywhere you go. I think it's unforgivable if artists start to abuse it."

Val likened a successful showbiz career to winning the pools.

"I do nothing more than stroll on stage, sing a few songs and have a chat with the audience. It's as simple as that and I've become very successful and quite wealthy for doing that. I was just a lad who started with little dance bands."

I count myself privileged to have been the first press man to have interviewed Val for as long as he can remember. He was clearly not an ego seeker and was more happy to stay in the background, despite the sheer magnitude of his stardom. Hence the reason he had normally fought off interviews.

With that I left him to stroll on stage, sing a few songs and chat up the audience. It may have looked easy but it took a great pro to carry it off.

CHAPTER 3

Tommy Cooper

IMAGINE MY EXCITEMENT when Sandown Pavilion announced they had booked the legendary Tommy Cooper for a two-week run. I knew Tommy did not do many straight interviews but I had friends who knew him. These included Shanklin's Sy and Isa Lyn, who had made some of his props and had a magic shop two miles from the theatre. The South Wight Borough Council staff also always went out of their way to help and regularly gave me scoops.

Tommy was not in the best of health during his visit. He had real leg problems and his fortnight ended up as just a week. I went to the show on the Monday night and interviewed Tommy in his dressing room. I sensed he was quite lonely and just before I left he asked me if I would come down on some other nights just for a chat. That proved a real pleasure and I took both friends and family down to meet him. I told my two young children they would never see the like of Tommy Cooper again.

On the final night he introduced me to a lady in his dressing room: "John, this is not my wife," said Tommy. I replied that I was delighted to meet any friend of his. I quickly sussed it was his girlfriend and decided not to breathe a word to anyone. I have a head full of secrets. Sadly, after Tommy's tragic death, she sold her story to the papers. I was saddened by that fact. Eventually, it all came out again via the television dramatisation of his life.

People have always asked me whether Tommy was funny off stage. He didn't really try to be but when I sat with him and saw his size 14 shoes I couldn't resist a smile.

For many years, Tommy was the most impersonated man on British television and he was certainly flattered by this honour. "A lot of them do it better than me," quipped Tommy, with that characteristic laugh.

He was thrilled to have finally travelled to the Isle of Wight. He'd been an apprentice shipwright at Hythe, near Southampton, and at that time he longed for that short trip across the Solent. While there, he was set to perform at a works show in the canteen. It was, luckily, a catastrophe and thereby shaped his future career.

"I was stood there with all my stage tricks ready when I got stage fright and couldn't speak. In my panic I knocked my props over and all the tricks went wrong. The audience just laughed and I haven't stopped for over 40 years."

Later NAAFI canteens and then Windmill audiences were exposed to the mad magician. Bottle parties were all the rage and he often never came on stage until three am. Sloshed or not they loved him. Eventually his major television breakthrough came on McDonald Hobley's *It's Magic* television show.

Tommy Cooper only had to walk on stage to make people laugh. During that Sandown week he had a gate on stage and he just kept walking through it and each time the punters laughed louder.

During his younger days, Tommy was a boxer and performed judo. As time went by he turned to doing simple serious magic tricks for his own amusement.

Millions will never forget the night our Tommy died on a live television show. Given the choice, it must have been the way he would have wanted to go.

CHAPTER 4

Liz Fraser

WHEN YOU WRITE to a theatrical agent, you never know quite what to expect. Sometimes they go out of their way to help, but others either completely ignore you or don't pass on your interview request. Liz Fraser's agent, Peter Charlesworth, went out of his way to oblige. I visited her home in Fulham and did not need to check the number of her house. I knew she had a Basset Hound and, sure enough, there was one sat outside. He barked and then left us to it.

I love real true professionals and Liz was certainly that and also prepared to speak her mind. This led to a fascinating hour or so. Initially, she advertised herself in The Stage newspaper and got a chance in repertory in Accrington, as an ASM, with a few small parts, at £4 ten shillings a week – and she saved money. Later she had quick non-speaking roles in BBC television productions, like walking past Peter Cushing with a tray in her hands. Her mother, who had an open all hours shop, used to watch them all on a small television. Sadly, as they were all live, Liz never saw them.

Liz also appeared in the very first ITV television soap, as Julie Perkins in *Sixpenny Corner*. She was also in the first live play ever featured on ITV and still remembers the audition.

"I had to walk through a door and stop on a cross on the floor. I did this three times and got the job. I always remember when the red or green lights came on we had to either speed up or slow down."

I wanted to find out about her appearances with Tony Hancock.

"Tony looked on me as a sort of lucky mascot and I appeared in a lot of his early television shows. I always remember my first speaking part. It was at a dance and he sort of nudged me with his foot to see if I would dance with him. I had to say 'who are you kicking, you great fat lump?' He liked what I did in his shows and we became mates.

"I loved him to bits but he was a troubled man and lacked complete confidence. Tony talked to me a lot. He thought Kenneth Williams was better than him, so he got rid of him and he didn't want to be a kind of double act with Sid James, so he went. Tony was his own worst enemy."

Later Liz had got to the stage in her career when she was doing too much comedy and she decided, with her agent, to come out of the Carry On movies.

"I might as well have been in every one, because I became so associated with them, which I bitterly resent. We never got paid well. I got £600 a film and no money for residuals. Poor Joan Sims, who worked so hard, died in very sad circumstances, without much money at all. She did ask the producer for a little bit of help, as there was no money for repeats, but was refused it. They were enjoyable to make, but are not good business memories."

Liz was seen in several memorable movies including *Two Way Stretch*, *I'm Alright Jack* and *Up The Junction*.

On the day of my visit, she was going for a costume meeting for a television appearance and apologised because she couldn't give me lunch. She suggested I had coffee and a couple of digestive biscuits to keep me going. Back she came with two biscuits on a plate surrounded by cheese, tomatoes and lettuce. What a lady!

CHAPTER 5

Joe Pasquale

WHEN ENTERTAINMENT managers, musicians and pros go out of their way to advise you to watch an act, it's time to take notice. In the case of Joe Pasquale, I certainly wasn't disappointed. I've never ever seen an act like it. He describes it as "cack." Whatever it is, it's funny and the punters thrive on it.

Joe was another Jim Davidson, in the respect that he was a runner-up in the grand final of *New Faces*. Unlike Jim, he didn't really have a stage act ready to capitalise on his sudden success. In fact, he was a Warner's greencoat at the time. Within a few years he had created an act that made him unique and spotlessly clean.

Joe has never forgotten his roots and has always enjoyed going back to holiday centres as the star attraction. With his innovative act there was precious little for the budding holiday centre entertainers to jot down. After he became really famous, Joe went back to read out the bingo numbers for an old mate at a small village holiday centre. He was announced as Billy Millett And His Dancing Chickweed. People were so surprised because he sounded just like Joe Pasquale – and some didn't realise it really was him.

At Warner's Corton Holiday Centre he got banned from taking the campers on a ramble. It was a small village and 400 joined him on the walk. He was dressed as Spiderman in wellington boots and they played havoc. They all visited the village shop, queued at the bus stop and hid behind a wall to surprise a lady who was cutting her roses. She ran indoors and nearly fainted. She turned out to be the Mayor's wife and there was trouble when they finally got back to the centre, after a few visits to the local pub.

When I first met Joe, back in 1992, at Warner's Bembridge Coast Hotel, he was virtually unknown but I knew he was a star in the making. He was such a refreshing character, both on and off stage. Every time I have met him since, in places like Cheltenham, Southampton, Shanklin and London, he never fails to ask about some of the cabaret acts who should have really made the big time. One of his greatest influences was an Isle of Wight-based, mad magician called Crisco, who was a visiting cabaret at some of the holiday centres he worked at. Numerous barmen even told me they saw Crisco's act every week and never failed to laugh.

In the early days Joe did skits on Johnny Mathis, with a burning candle routine, and Michael Jackson, among others. Being so inventive, he never failed to impress. None of us could have imagined he would end up starring in West End plays and musicals, hosting game shows like *The Price Is Right* and stealing a Royal Variety Show with Des O'Connor and a camel.

Was recording four game shows in a day hard work? "It was a lot easier than walking around Smithfield Meat Market, humping great lumps of meat on my back."

Joe gave me a real scare on one occasion when he told me he had flown a plane over the Isle of Wight. I thought it was a gag but he was deadly serious and had qualified as a pilot. With both him and Bradley Walsh flying around it was a daunting thought.

He also looked back on the TV programme *I'm A Celebrity... Get Me Out Of Here* with great satisfaction. Winning it gave his career another boost and introduced him to a whole new audience.

Interviewing Joe is an experience in itself and you never quite know what he's got in store for you. Amazingly, he once did two theatre shows at Newport's Medina Theatre, despite the revived Isle of Wight Music Festival being in the field next door. He still sold out both performances.

CHAPTER 6

Mandy Rice-Davies

EVEN BEFORE Mandy Rice-Davies became the world's most famous 18-year-old in 1963, she was a teenager with a difference. Her idols were Albert Schweitzer, Colonel Harry Llewellyn, Clark Gable and Winston Churchill – and she wanted to be a missionary.

"I didn't become a missionary, I became Mandy Rice-Davies – a little different," she reflected, when I caught up with her backstage at the Kings Theatre, Southsea, in 1985.

Our get together had been arranged by a lovely old radio comedian called Tony Scott, who had made hundreds of appearances on the wireless, as we used to call it. When I saw he was touring Britain in a *Bedfull Of Foreigners*, with Mandy Rice-Davies, an interview opportunity loomed. Always ready to please, Tony duly fixed it all up and it happened to be on my birthday – what a present!

Not many people realised they had heard Mandy long before the Profumo affair. She had been the queen of the television commercials, with her most famous being: "You wonder where the yellow went when you clean your teeth with Pepsodent." There were others and she also appeared in the British movie *Make Mine Mink* and was seen in the *Sammy Davis Jr Show*.

Then, suddenly, in 1963 everybody knew her name. They say all publicity is good publicity. Mandy was still in demand in 1985. In a way, it was ample proof. How did she feel two decades on?

"It all happened, it was there and I accepted it. I'm not sure if it was good. Where would I be today, I don't know? Probably in a pantomime."

Not surprisingly, Mandy took to the hills and became a cabaret singer in Germany. The offer of £1000 a week in 1964 was too good to refuse. She had barely a week to prepare.

It was rather difficult for her to know exactly what to do after that little bit of bother in '63. "I had to work and decide how to handle myself."

The world's press from *Time Magazine* downwards turned up at that German cabaret debut. Mandy continued her showbiz career that had begun back in 1960. She made movies at home and abroad and readily admitted many were rubbish. There was a West End season, several theatre tours around Britain and a television spot in *Birds Of Prey*. While living in Israel for a time, she worked at the Hebrew National Theatre and owned a few Chinese restaurants.

She also had written her autobiography and a romantic novel or two.

"I am a great romantic and that's why I've been married a few times. Falling in love is wonderful. It's the only black magic available to everyone and doesn't cost any money."

Mandy was very much a part of one of the great decades of the past 50 years but, in fact, knew very little about the '60s. Well, she admitted to have left a bit quick.

"I didn't hit the swinging London part. Mind you, it was a bit swinging before 1963."

After the matinee performance at the Kings Theatre, Southsea, the company left us to it and we were chatting together in the dressing room. Then we headed to the transport cafe next door. Mandy ordered an egg on toast and went and sat on the same table as a lorry driver. He had no idea who she was. Twenty two years earlier it would have been a dream come true and a story to dine out on forever.

CHAPTER 7

Benny Hill

IN LATE SEPTEMBER 1989, I had a call from an Isle of Wight-based showbiz agent called Sylvia Thorley, inviting me to her end-of-season party for all the artists that had worked for her that summer. I had interviewed quite a few of them. I was so shocked when she told me Benny Hill would be coming, as a special guest. I didn't think this would happen but, just in case, I put my trusted cassette recorder in the car boot. I arrived – and there was Benny.

Sylvia, who had supplied some Hill's Angels for Benny's television shows, had a quick chat with him and he readily agreed to an instant interview. It was the perfect scenario. Benny was sat at a table, surrounded by beautiful young ladies, and was in his element. With an attentive audience, he gave me a brilliant interview.

At that time Benny was living, rather modestly, in Southampton. I contacted their local evening paper, *The Echo*, to see if they were interested in a feature on him. They jumped at the offer, as he wouldn't talk to them. It was published as a full page spread. With the *Isle of Wight Weekly Post* also using the story, it was an unexpected double. A few years later, the cassette recording was used as an archive on my local radio show.

Benny suddenly revealed a fascinating story of how Danny Kaye had saved his ailing showbiz career. He was on the brink of returning to Southampton to become a part-time musician in a local dance band.

"I'd really made up my mind to quit the business and as it was cheaper by coach than train to Southampton, I was forced to wait in London until six o'clock. I went into the Bijou Cinema, in Victoria, to watch a Danny Kaye film, called *Wonder Man*.

"I came out inspired and thinking, if he can do it, so can I," reflected Benny, who never got on that coach.

With his television shows seen in 90 countries, including Russia, China and Japan, Benny became as world famous as the celluloid superstar who had changed his mind.

By choice, Benny lived a life far removed from his superstar image. He didn't drive a car, owned a very small house and did his own shopping. It was also clear he hated the national press.

"They write so many crap things about me and they're all made up. There have been stories about my shopping list, eating habits, villas in France and Spain and cost-saving holidays in Hornchurch. None of them had an atom of truth.

" I don't spend as much on myself as Robert Maxwell or Rupert Murdoch, but I spend more than someone like Mother Teresa does. Am I on the side of the angels or the devil?

"Because I don't spend much on myself doesn't necessarily mean I don't spend it on someone else or give it away," said Benny.

It was a real break with tradition for Benny to even talk to the press and I was so flattered to be given the rare honour. I didn't overstay my welcome and thoroughly enjoyed his company.

Just before I left, Benny was keen to put one regular misnomer well and truly straight.

"I don't like being accused of always chasing people at the end of my television shows. If you look closely, I'm always the one being chased."

Benny is pictured with Sylvia Thorley at the Lincoln Hotel, Shanklin, in 1989. Sadly, they are no longer with us. I have fond memories of both of them.

CHAPTER 8

Frankie Howerd

THE POSSIBILITY of not even getting an interview with Frankie Howerd caused me a few sleepless nights. Having been a self-confessed fan for many years, the thought of him virtually performing on my own doorstep seemed too good to be true. Some pessimists even suggested one of my lifetime ambitions would remain just that. I bet they were surprised when the great comic took my wife and myself out to dinner.

Some comedians are never off stage. I have met a few who have been funnier off than on. There are some who are so keyed up they even do 20 minutes when the fridge door opens and the light comes on. Away from the spotlight, Frankie Howerd never created that laugh-a-minute image. In fact, he was rather on the shy side but interviewing him was immensely enjoyable. Naturally, there were the inevitable titters. No please – don't mock Francis! It was hard to believe he was once a Sunday school teacher.

At the age of 13 Frankie played Tilly's father in a local production of *Tilly Of Bloomsbury* and had been coached word for word. He got rave reviews and a church warden suggested he should become an actor. He did eventually get a chance at RADA but was thrown out because he stuttered. It didn't enhance Shakespeare, unfortunately.

"When I heard the bad news I went into a field near my home and cried for an hour, sobbing my heart out. Then I decided to show a bit of courage and there and then decided, as I was not going to rival Sir Laurence Olivier, to become a comic."

That led to an amazing career which probably culminated, in most people's eyes, in those epic *Up Pompeii!* television shows. There were many other highs and a few lows which he fought back from. A *Funny Thing Happened On The Way To The Forum* was another outstanding moment.

Frankie tried to convince me he was not a great worrier. He blamed interviewers for creating that image.

"People interview me and it's nice for them to have something to talk about. So this subject crops up. It's what you're doing now. Everyone who is conscientious worries. Ours is a profession where you have to take trouble. When I was a youngster I worked like mad to do it properly," said Frankie.

My wife and I were invited out to a Frankie Howerd post-show dinner, along with his pianist, Madame Dixon, and his manager. It was all very quiet and needed a take off point. I had an idea and mentioned tennis, his great love. I talked about the recent epic Wimbledon final between Borg and McEnroe – and with that he never stopped talking for the rest of the evening.

On that night, at a cliff top restaurant, he asked Heather what I was like at home and she revealed a few secrets, much to his delight. Then he stunned me by asking if I ever thought about dying. It was a fantastic evening that I will never forget. You could just never guess the next conversation topic.

As we left the Culver Down restaurant, which was around 1.30am, he put his arm around my shoulder and asked if I knew anything about stars. I suggested I'd just had dinner with one. He then pointed skywards and rattled off some amazing constellations, which would have impressed Patrick Moore. My interest in stars was more at ground level.

Frankie did ask me for one real favour. En route from an Australian tour he'd lost his cassette copy of a James Last album that contained *The Lonely Shepherd* tune. That was easy to rectify. I hope he didn't lose it going home on the ferry.

CHAPTER 9

Britt Ekland

PANTOMIME STARS from the Mayflower Theatre, Southampton, have always been a joy to interview. I have only ever been turned down by one person from their star studded line-ups of the past 40 years or more. That was Lily Savage. Britt Ekland certainly said yes.

I arrived early and was given a message to say she was running late. I was more than happy to wait. Britt arrived backstage and I was ushered into her dressing room. What was this world famous blonde going to look like? I was totally shocked to find a lady with black hair waiting to see me. I said nothing other than to introduce myself. Her first words to me were: "I suppose you want to talk about Peter Sellers like everyone else." She seemed surprised when I said I didn't, but not enough to stop painting her fingernails. Actually, I had no intention of asking her anything about him or any of the other men in her life.

I only do face-to-face interviews but, on this occasion, it was face-to-fingernails, as she never looked up. She talked enthusiastically about her career and the role of a pantomime baddie. A couple of days later I went to my hair stylist (I had hair in those days), Tracey Squibb, of Hairleaders, Newport, Isle of Wight, and she could barely wait to ask me about Britt and, in particularly, her famous blonde hair. When I told her she had black hair when I interviewed her, Tracey thought I'd finally lost the plot. Too many interviews had addled my brain. A few days later my Sunday studio host for my live two-hour radio chat show, an enthusiastic young lady called Jess Snazell, came up with the perfect reason as to why Miss Ekland had black hair. She explained that Britt was probably still wearing her black street wig. What a perfect disguise for a famous blonde.

The next time I met Britt was in 2010 at the Kings Theatre, Southsea, when she was again in pantomime. When the rehearsals had begun she was 10,000 miles away in an Australian TV jungle. The day I saw the show for *The Stage* newspaper was her first appearance, following her jet flight from Down Under. I had a problem. I quickly realised she didn't know the script or her stage entrances and exits. I knew she would soon pick these up and decided not to mention them in my review. I was interviewing her after the show, but this was wearing my other hat.

This time out she was much more friendly and actually had blonde hair. Being just in from *I'm A Celebrity... Get Me Out Of Here!* it was certainly newsworthy. She didn't regret doing the programme and lasted 16 days.

"When you work as an actress you always say that you made lots of friends on your last production. The jungle is a different form of attachment. It's very raw and highly emotional. It's nothing to do with going out and having a drink after the show. Your relationship with everyone is about surviving. So you learn to rely and trust each other. I made some incredible friends at that level in the jungle."

What of the press coverage of a kind of spat with Gillian McKeith? "I don't wish to give that unmentionable person any more publicity than she's had already. I am glad Stacey Solomon won it."

I had to mention *The Man With The Golden Gun*. "Being a Bond girl, and I still am, has been an incredible experience. It's a role people will always remember you for."

CHAPTER 10

Bradley Walsh

I'D SEEN BRADLEY WALSH work in holiday centres long before he became famous. The first time I interviewed him was at Warner's, Norton Grange, Yarmouth. By the time I met him again, this time at Warner's, Bembridge, in 2007, he was a real household name, having appeared in so many television shows, including a stint in *Coronation Street*.

I knew Bradley would be late at the venue because earlier in the day he was flying back to England from Dubai. The centre's bandleader Doug Watson always kept me informed of what was happening. I never expected to get an opportunity, but Doug rang to say Bradley had just arrived and if I was quick he would see me before going on stage. My gear was already in the car boot.

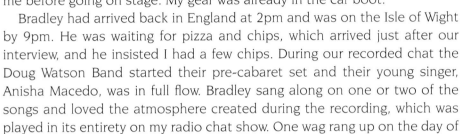

Bradley had arrived back in England at 2pm and was on the Isle of Wight by 9pm. He was waiting for pizza and chips, which arrived just after our interview, and he insisted I had a few chips. During our recorded chat the Doug Watson Band started their pre-cabaret set and their young singer, Anisha Macedo, was in full flow. Bradley sang along on one or two of the songs and loved the atmosphere created during the recording, which was played in its entirety on my radio chat show. One wag rang up on the day of transmission and suggested Bradley Walsh was drowning the singer out – and who was she? There's always one!

Bradley, Joe Pasquale and Darren Day were among the unknown acts who played the Warner centres before they became star names.

"People like Joe and myself were against each other in talent shows during the early days and then we progressed as young comics. At the time we thought wouldn't it be nice if the older guys like Bruce Forsyth, Des O'Connor and Jimmy Tarbuck moved over to give us a chance.

"It's not really like that at all. There is room for everybody and you rub shoulders with the established stars. Probably now young entertainers are wanting Joe and I to move over to give them a chance," said Bradley.

In fact the greats like Forsyth, Tarbuck and O'Connor did give the young comics like Bradley a chance on their major television shows.

Bradley was very shrewd and could sense the light entertainment scene was slowly dying and that the game shows did not need performers any more. Then he was given some advice by Ray Winstone.

"Ray was a friend of mine and told me to forget what I had been doing and move into acting. I took his advice and was glad I did,"

Bradley eventually joined *Coronation Street* as Danny Baldwin and loved the experience. Millions enjoyed his portrayal of Ronnie Brooks in over 50 episodes of *Law and Order*: UK. Proving he was a genuine all-rounder he became a cult figure on *The Chase* and as the host of *Tonight At The London Palladium* introduced both new and established acts.

During our last interview Bradley asked me to play one of Neil Sedaka's greatest ever songs, *The Hungry Years*.

"I love the words of that Sedaka song. In fact sometimes I cast my mind back to the early days when life was tough and you always travelled on your own. There was something about those hungry years when you were striving for success."

Bradley, like Joe Pasquale and Shane Richie, also asks me about a local entertainer called Chris Cox, who worked as Crisco. Chris, who should have been a star, impressed them in their early days with his innovative comedy and was a great inspiration. "He was too far ahead of his time and the TV companies didn't know what to do with him," added Bradley.

CHAPTER 11

Roger De Courcey

LIKE MILLIONS OF OTHERS I enjoyed the success of Nookie Bear and Roger de Courcey on *New Faces* and those subsequent shows that included *The Royal Variety Performance*. I met them for the first time at the now defunct Warner's Holiday Centre at Woodside Bay and Roger was in the process of doing 12 shows in seven days. He spared me a few minutes before his cabaret spot – and for once he did more talking than Nookie. I was not so lucky on two other occasions but more of that later.

Twenty minutes after our interview I had so much sympathy for Roger. A punter decided to play on the fruit machine right in the middle of his act and we all cheered when, in the voice of Nookie, he told the guy just what to go and do.

Ironically, 17 years earlier Roger had been a sports organiser in a holiday centre, but in 1979 was touring as a visiting cabaret star, with a very lucrative contract. At that time holiday centres could also regularly boast of star turns like Ted Rogers, Roy Hudd, Vince Hill and Dukes and Lee.

Prior to the Isle of Wight date, Roger had appeared on the Friday night for a national company in Portsmouth, the following day was at Caesar's Palace, Luton, then he headed for a Sunday night in the Isle of Man and then it was back to the Isle of Wight for two Monday night gigs in Wootton and Yarmouth.

He told me; "This goes on all summer. I'm earning a lot of money and I hope to live to enjoy it."

Long before *New Faces* was conceived Roger had studied opera and had appeared in West End shows like *Sweet Charity*, *Two Cities* and *Company*.

"After five years in the West End and becoming the eternal understudy it seemed I would never get a real chance. I thought it was time for a change and became a ventriloquist."

Suddenly Nookie came to life and added: "He's not really one of those either." Roger instantly joked: "I have been voted the world's worst vent."

His very first bear was bought for one shilling at a jumble sale. From that cupboard at Stoney Stratford and Roger's self-taught lessons, Nookie finally arrived on the scene.

I wish this story had a happy ending but far from it. When Roger came to Sandown Pavilion a few years later he promised me an interview and told me to wait at the stage door. I was there on time and when he came out he just ignored me completely, said nothing and walked away.

Then a year or two later he was booked for a star cabaret spot at Warner's Norton Grange, at Yarmouth. I wrote a nice letter to his agent and had a curt reply stating that Mr de Courcey was not interested at all in doing an interview.

I went to the show and all was not well. Roger had thought it was an adults only audience and when he came on stage you could see the fear in his eyes when he saw 50 children sat at the edge of the cabaret floor. For two reasons, I didn't feel sorry for him at all.

CHAPTER 12

Melvyn Hayes

WHEN THE CLIFF RICHARD movies like *The Young Ones* and *Summer Holiday* suddenly appeared on our cinema screens they brought a whole new dimension to British film musicals, particularly those that featured pop stars. Films like *It's Trad Dad* and *Just For Fun* had weak story lines and were overcrowded with pop singers of the day. It was not only Cliff who made this new era of screen musicals so popular. His strong supporting cast included talented young actors like Melvyn Hayes.

I first met Melvyn at the end of one of the busiest weeks he'd ever had in his 30-year career. It was 1980 and both he and Windsor Davies, his co-star in TV's hit series *It Ain't Half Hot Mum*, starred in an Isle of Wight summer season at the Shanklin Theatre. Their play was called *Sink Or Swim* and it's not been revived too often since then.

At the time I had my *Stage Talk* column in the local *Weekly Post* newspaper. My intention, to help publicise their show, was to interview one at the start of their six- week season and the other one halfway through, to spread the publicity. Melvyn readily accepted and gave me a wonderful interview. Windsor turned me down a couple of times during the run and I never got to talk to him. Years later in a huge Southampton Mayflower pantomime, he was one of six stars to give me a ten-minute interview for my radio show. He was so good and I went back the next week to do a 30 minute interview with him.

Back to that summer of 1980 and the lack of sleep that fame can bring. It was amazing that Melvyn even managed to stay awake during our interview.

"This first week would have driven a nine to five working man almost insane. After a few hours sleep, following the show, I would wake Windsor at 5.30am. We said good morning to the birds, who coughed back to us, and then drove 11 miles to Cowes to catch the early ferry to Southampton. We had breakfast on the London train and then headed to the rehearsals for the final episode of the current series of *It Ain't Half Hot Mum*. Then around teatime we headed back to Shanklin for the evening performance.

"Thankfully the final episode is in the can. In one scene I was supposed to be asleep - and I think I really was."

How times had changed for Melvyn. A few years earlier he'd been earning £9 a week in the play *Change For The Angel* at a London theatre club. He couldn't even afford to buy food but was rather clever.

"In the first scene I took a Coca Cola and fruit cake from a cupboard. In the second I had a meal of mash potato, salad and sausages and in the third a bowl of fruit was placed on the table. My only food was on stage. On Saturdays and Sundays we had two shows but on Mondays we didn't work, so I starved."

Millions loved Melvyn's creation of Gloria in *It Ain't Half Hot Mum* and there was no doubt that he stole an episode on several occasions.

Over 20 years on from his summer season there were rumours that Melvyn had moved to the Isle of Wight. I managed to contact him but he wanted to lay low for a while. Eventually he consented to a radio interview and I had a job to stop him talking. From that day we have become good friends and now occasionally meet socially. He and his wife, Jayne, are such good company. We even did a charity gig together at a local theatre and he was in great form, despite feeling unwell in the interval.

CHAPTER 13

James Last

JAMES LAST brought big band music to a whole generation of new fans who were excited by the release of stereo LPs to play on their trendy new radiograms. I still remember buying This Is James Last, a vinyl sampler album, which must have sold millions of copies worldwide. We took some friends to one of his first British tours and joined the packed house at the Bournemouth Winter Gardens.

The orchestra were fantastic and it certainly was a day and night to remember. We were booked on the 3am car ferry from Portsmouth to the Isle of Wight and went for a meal before we left Bournemouth. Whilst we were waiting I decided to check on the closing time of the car park – and it had long past. After the meal we headed back to the car park and discovered there was a way out, as they were rebuilding part of it. The gap was small but we put the car rug along the wooden fence to avoid scratches and somehow got out.

A few years later in 1999 I decided to try and interview James at a Bank Holiday gig at the Mayflower, Southampton. I put in a request and got a reply from his PR lady in America. It was the first day of the tour but it might be possible if I turned up around teatime. We left home with no idea if I had the interview and with no tickets for the show, as it had been sold out for months. I had all my recording gear and the covers of 16 James Last albums.

They had finished their rehearsals and soundchecks and James could spare me around 30 minutes. Whilst I was setting up he signed all the vinyl LP covers and then we recorded our interview. He was in fine form and very friendly.

"John after you have packed up your equipment please take the lift to the top of the theatre and join us for a cup of tea," suggested James.

We arrived and all the chairs were taken by the huge orchestra but there were spare seats on James' table and he called us over, so we took our paper cups and joined them. Then he asked if we had eaten. If not, would we like to have a meal with them. We hadn't and this was proving an exciting day. He then asked if we were going to the concert. We had to tell him we couldn't get tickets.

"That will not be a problem. You can join my girlfriend and doctor in my party and be my guests," insisted James.

We were so grateful but I had to be honest. I told him we had to catch the last ferry home to Cowes and might have to leave just before the end. If he happened to spot us leaving it wouldn't be because we weren't enjoying the show. We managed to slip away quietly just a few minutes before the end of the fantastic show.

On the way home I remembered an amazing story that I had written many years earlier in my weekly showbiz column in the local weekly tabloid. On the Isle of Wight, the British Hovercraft Corporation held a very prestigious ball every year and they always had a star British band, like those of Ken Macintosh and Bob Miller. Obviously, a real greenhorn booker fancied the Germany-based James Last Orchestra and even made an enquiry. The cost, in 1978, for the one night would have been £26,000.

CHAPTER 14

John Mills

THERE ARE DAYS IN YOUR LIFE that you will never forget. In my case, going to the Denham Village home of Sir John Mills was such an occasion. I arrived early and just sat in my car outside of his wonderful cottage, feeling my heart pounding with excitement. I was going to meet a true legend of the movies – and he was one of our own.

On a pure whim, I decided to write to Sir John to ask for an interview. During my 40 plus years of meeting famous people I've always been prepared to try – and it's no, anyway, until you ask.

Sir John's PA rang me to say she had read him my letter, he'd liked it and I was very welcome to come to his home.

When I rang the bell at his cottage, I heard a rather surprised voice saying that the door had not been locked the night before. That was a little worrying with a house full of personal treasures. I was given such a warm welcome and then the news that Sir John had just had his back massaged and had fallen asleep. They assured me it wouldn't be too long a wait. I was just happy to meet his staff, play with the dogs and enjoy my coffee.

Suddenly, I heard an unmistakable voice and began to tingle all over - and the hair I had left seemed to stand up on end. "Now this young man's name is John, isn't it. I can't forget that," said one of my all-time favourite movie stars, who was stood right behind me. He readily agreed to a 45 minute interview and warned me that he might take a carrot juice halfway through.

We really hit it off, but all of a sudden he stopped me – and I feared the worst. He said: "John I must congratulate you because you know more about John Mills than I do," which I took as a real compliment. Apparently, the week before he'd been interviewed by a young lady journalist from a trendy magazine who'd done no research at all. Her

opening words were: "So, Sir John, tell me what you've done in your life." He was not amused.

There was so much to talk about and he had so many wonderful stories of legendary movies and, of course, his friendship with the one and only Noel Coward. Such a modest man without even an ounce of arrogance. I had encountered a few young soap stars with huge egos, prior to meeting Sir John, and they weren't even fit to clean his shoes.

How did his chance come in movies?

"I was rather lucky. In 1932 when I was appearing in Noel Coward's *Words And Music* at the Adelphi Theatre, they wanted a young actor who could sing and dance for the movie *The Midshipmaid*, opposite the great star Jesse Matthews, so I didn't have to audition for the part. At that time, West End actors looked down on movies and said they were only doing them for the money. I didn't feel that way. I loved the studios. It was difficult but I loved the challenge," said Sir John. It was a wise decision, as he appeared in well over 100 films.

My favourite story is from *Ryan's Daughter*, when Sir John won an Oscar for his portrayal of Michael, the deaf and dumb mute.

"At the ceremony I told the audience I was delighted but had been wasting my time all along, as I got it for not talking.

"I had worked on the part beforehand but during the filming, while they were sweating over learning their lines, I was drinking Guinness in the pub."

CHAPTER 15

Les Reed

MY UNEXPECTED OPPORTUNITY to interview Les Reed was entirely due to pop singer Craig Douglas, a fellow caulkhead. In other words – born on the Isle of Wight. He was in a play with Les and asked the hit songwriter if he could send me one of his career brochures. I was impressed and Craig did the rest and a few months later I ended up at his lovely country house and drove in through the first electronic gates I'd ever seen.

Now I was really excited. I had been such a fan of the John Barry Seven, for whom Les had played piano, and loved his electrifying Pop Proms television spectaculars, when he fronted a huge orchestra. They also had genuine world stars on the show. My lifelong love of songwriters also meant I knew so many of his hits.

As ever, I wondered what he would be like. Within five minutes I was in the kitchen drinking coffee and Les and his wife June were the perfect hosts.

It was a day to remember. We talked for over an hour about all aspects of his amazing career and I was fascinated with his tales of the John Barry Seven. It was a two-hour radio special and I had a problem even before I arrived. How could I possibly fit all of his world famous songs into the show? I could easily fill it with the gems he penned for Tom Jones and Englebert Humperdinck. It all worked well in the end and I even found a place for part of his soundtrack from the very sexy Marianne Faithfull movie *The Girl On A Motorcycle*.

Les and I really had fun and just before I left he told me it would be a pleasure for him to fix up other interviews with some of his musical associates and mates. Just give me a ring, suggested Les.

A few weeks later I was in the car and listening to a Matt Monro tribute show, around the tenth anniversary of his tragic death, presented by none other than Don Black. I decided to ring Les and ask if he could arrange an interview with Don. Two days later I was in the loft when my phone rang and it was Don Black. Les had struck gold and had set it up so perfectly. I even found out Don had died a death as a comedian in a gig at the Commodore, Ryde. A few years later some of his great songs were being sung by Matt, at the same venue. In Don's wake came Barry Mason, Geoff Stephens, Roger Cook and Tony Macaulay. Dare I ask Les for a world superstar?

Emails had arrived on the scene by then and I sent one to Les asking how one went about trying to get an interview with Englebert. Following a few transatlantic emails I was promised an interview the next time Enge came home to Britain. It really happened and I spent over two hours at his Leicester home. I never had the courage to ask Les about the great Tom Jones.

I went back to record a second radio special with Les and it proved so popular. What a talented guy and not a hint of self importance. Just a genuine nice man. In the 26 years of my long running radio show I tried to play as many Les Reed songs as I could. From *Delilah* to *That's What Life Is All About* via *The Last Waltz* and *There's A Kind Of Hush*. In this business you have to help one another. I still enjoy so many of his fantastic CD releases.

CHAPTER 16

Barbara Windsor

BACK IN 1988, I interviewed Barbara Windsor – and this was long before Albert Square. Her parting shot to me in the Cowes Corinthian Yacht Club, which is slightly more upmarket than the Queen Vic, was a possible hint of her future direction.

"I never liked being a part of a team. I just wanted to be on my own. Now I'm older, I'd rather like to be a part of a team.

"As you get older, the confidence stops and you need familiar faces around you. It would be nice to be in a soap and see the same faces every Monday morning."

Barbara and Gareth Hunt came to the Isle of Wight to attend the Stone's Ginger J 24 yachting championship. They both also took part in a tin bath race.

Those were the days when you could just turn up at an event attended by a few stars and virtually get an instant interview. There were no PR people to block your path or wind-up your interview after just a few minutes. We also had real stars and not mindless celebs.

At the time Barbara was 50 and simply fed up with being offered the parts of 30-year-olds. Some ladies would have been so envious. "I just want to play someone my own age. The Carry On image has been hard to live down," said Barbara.

We hit it off instantly and she told me it was nice to meet an interviewer more interested in her professional life than her private life – and told me why.

"The national tabloids have tried to make me a personality, which I rather resent. I've not been able to get on with my job. I'm a working actress.

"Suddenly they weren't writing about my acting, just my private life. This is still with me and I don't like it very much," said Barbara, who admitted a fear of picking up the morning papers.

Thankfully her true fans stayed loyal and this had proved a great comfort to her.

Babs, as she is affectionately known, was spotted at a charity concert given by her convent school. It was big-time impresario Brian Michie who liked the look of her.

"He said I'd got something – and I didn't have the boobs in those days," reflected Barbara.

With her father a bus driver and mother a dressmaker, it was hard to follow the advice to send her to a theatre school. In the end, she went to Aida Foster for a term. At the age of 14 she was in the West End's *Love From Judy*, at the Saville Theatre. Amazingly, before spending those two years on a London stage she had no real desire to go into the theatre.

"This might surprise you. I had wanted to be a nun and then a foreign language telephonist." Imagine Miss Windsor in a habit!

Like many others, who developed into fine actors, she spent some early days at the Stratford East Theatre with Joan Littlewood. Among her contemporaries there were Brian Murphy and Lionel Bart. It was Bart's *Fings Ain't Wot They Used To Be* that proved to be the turning point in her stage career. During nearly three years in that show she was also seen on TV's *The Rag Trade* and, hence, often spotted on London trains.

"Most people associate me with Carry On films, but really they have played a minor part in my career. That's the power of television. They've been cut up and used in so many programmes."

At that time she would sooner have been remembered for her creations of Marie Lloyd, Lucy Brown in the *Threepenny Opera* and Maria in *Twelfth Night*.

Twice in later years I tried to interview Barbara again, with no success.

CHAPTER 17

Alan Freeman

I FIRST MET ALAN FREEMAN right back in the late '50s when he used to compère those wonderful pop package tours and I was proud to have obtained his autograph. I can remember going to a Craig Douglas concert at the Guildhall, Portsmouth, and enjoying a running gag from 'Fluff', as the screaming girls got even more excited. He told them that coming on later, as Craig's surprise guest star, was a guy with the initials AF. They made up their own minds and presumed that it would be a certain Adam Faith, who just happened to be top of the hit parade at the time. It wasn't, of course, and on walked another AF – Alan Freeman.

Fifty years later Craig was my link to finally interviewing Alan. I'd found out that he was now a resident at Brinsworth House, in Twickenham, the retirement home for entertainers. Craig had performed a cabaret spot there and had asked Alan on my behalf. Many years earlier they had shared the same agents, Bunny Lewis and Janique Joelle.

I arrived at Brinsworth and was a wee bit early for my afternoon rendezvous with Alan. I was actually met at the door by the man himself, with the words: "Hi John boy! I'm still eating my lunch but I saw you coming up the drive. You go and sit in the bar, where there are some nice cosy chairs."

The staff were very friendly and one lady told me she was Ruby Murray's sister.

Then I saw Alan approaching with a tray in his hands. "While you're waiting I've brought you some cherries and custard. I expect you can polish them off." How right he was. We had coffee and then headed for his room. It was called The Max Bygraves Room. Some of the stars had donated a room to Brinsworth. Strangely, there was not a pink toothbrush in sight!

I love stories from the early lives of famous people and Alan had plenty to relate. The interview was planned to last an hour and form a two-hour special with music from his life.

Music was Alan's great love in his native Australia. After life as a cycling messenger boy with a chemical firm, he went on to work in the accounts office of a timber firm. Amazingly, for two years he trained as an opera singer.

"I was a baritone of sorts and was okay until I decided to listen to my own voice. I recorded myself singing two arias from La Traviata and was so disappointed that I wanted to commit suicide. That was the end of my opera world."

Thankfully, a friend introduced him to radio and he ended up with the 7LA station in Tasmania and then 3KZ in Melbourne. He was around 27 and restless, so he decided to tour the world for a few months.

"I arrived in London on April 1, 1957, and could barely wait to turn on the BBC. It was like the Vatican and Buckingham Palace to me. They were playing Come Fly With Me by Frank Sinatra and the DJ said: 'Well that was Frank Sinatra on a gramophone record, with an orchestra led by Nelson Riddle.'

"I nearly fell off my stool as I couldn't believe what I was hearing. I thought, of course, he's on a record. He hasn't flown in from LA to sing one bleeding song."

When Alan got the job with the BBC he went in with all guns blazing – and never looked back. Our 'Fluff' became a national treasure.

As a parting shot, he recorded a personal jingle for my show. "Is that okay John boy?" I replied: "Not 'alf!"

CHAPTER 18

Bob Monkhouse

BOB MONKHOUSE first discovered summer season shows during some 1930s family holidays on the Isle of Wight. Fifty years later he finally emulated some of his earliest comedy idols from those shows, which included Arthur Askey, Eric Barker and Dickie Hassett. Bob topped the bill at Sandown Pavilion in the summer of 1988.

"On those schoolboy holidays in the '30s the one highlight for me was going to the summer shows. I saw Arthur Askey at Shanklin's Summer Theatre in 1936, when he was virtually still unknown, and Eric Barker a year later at Sandown Pavilion. I loved watching the top of the bill comics," reflected Bob, during our very first interview, which was to prove the start of a friendship.

In 2000 I published my very first book, I *Was A Stage Door Johnny*. I wanted someone famous to write the foreword. I'd got to know Bob well and decided to ring his agent, the legendary Peter Pritchard, whom I had so much respect for, as he'd proved so helpful with interview requests for his star studded array of artists.

Peter, ever the gentleman, was very courteous but warned that Bob normally doesn't do that type of thing and it probably would not happen, but he would ask him. A couple of nights later Bob rang me at home to say he would be delighted to write the foreword. I was so thrilled and was really flattered by his words.

On several occasions I willingly offered to be Bob's driver when he returned for one nighters and a later short summer season in Ryde. Once I went to pick him up from his hotel and he asked to sit in the back seat. He was wearing a real classy suit. After I'd dropped him off I suddenly realised my two young people had been eating chocolate in the back seat of the car earlier that day and the evidence was clearly still visible. Had Bob sat in that exact spot? I never had the courage to ask him when we next met.

Bob Monkhouse (top) with Wally Malston

A year or two later Bob came into the Isle of Wight Radio studio to record an interview with me. I had picked him up and was also going to run him back to his posh country hotel after the show. En route to the Swainston Hotel he asked me to stop at a small village shop for him to do a little shopping. I sat in the car and he finally came out with his Spar carrier bag. I went into the store a few days later and they asked me to guess the famous TV star who'd been into their shop. They were amazed when I suggested Bob Monkhouse and the owner said: "How did you ever know that?" I had to admit I'd been sat in the car park waiting for him.

I have so many happy memories of knowing Bob and his lovely wife Jackie. When he did the final week of his 1988 Sandown summer season I went down every night to see him perform – and he changed his act every night. That was a real star for you.

I also arranged a reunion between Bob and one of his former scriptwriters, Wally Malston, who grew up on the Isle of Wight. Wally, a dental mechanic by trade, was brilliant with topical one-liners. He began by writing jokes for Bob when he hosted *Sunday Night At The London Palladium*. Wally was still in the dental trade at that time and Bob paid him £5 for every gag he used on Sunday nights. He ticked them off as he watched the show.

CHAPTER 19

Edward Windsor

IN 1998, I RECEIVED a press release from Meridian Television, who had been so kind to me over the years, with regard to *Crown And Country*. Their new series was being launched at Petworth House, near Chichester. Edward Windsor, the show's presenter, would be attending the event. I boldly asked for an in-person interview and was told it might be possible.

We arrived at Petworth House on a beautiful autumn day and I was told the interview was on. There were around 15 south coast journalists in the press conference room. We were briefed before Edward arrived and told three specific subjects we were not allowed to ask him about. It became very embarrassing when a lady from Kent asked him about all three. Thankfully, Edward handled it so well.

After the general press conference, Edward was to be interviewed by Meridian's Peter Henley and I was due to follow this, which was for my Isle of Wight Radio chat show. My wife and I were ushered into a very small room which was a mock bygone kitchen. Their chief press officer told us Edward was now running late as his Meridian interview had overrun.

Suddenly Edward burst into the room with his detective, who took one look at us and decided we looked harmless enough – and left. So the three of us were alone in this tiny room. I'd set up my equipment and during the interview, from the way we were positioned, neither Edward or myself could see the open door. I had been promised 10 minutes and decided to get just that. Unbeknown to me, after around three minutes the press officer gave Heather the wind-up signal. She had been brought up the right way – and ignored it. When my recorder clock had registered ten minutes I ended the interview. I quickly thanked him and asked him to choose a piece of music to end his spot. He called his detective back in to help him. I'd kept the machine running and Edward came up with an unexpected choice. "As you come from the Isle of Wight and we talked about the programme filmed there, why don't you play I'*ll Remember You* by Frank Ifield?" All of us, including Edward, burst out laughing.

I must say how impressed I was with Edward's role in *Crown And Country*. As the host of the show he fronted it so well with an amazing knowledge of each location. At the time he had his own company, Ardent Productions, and he definitely could have had a real future in the media. In the show devoted to the Isle of Wight, he talked about things I never even knew about – and I was born there. One of my local country runs was past Appuldurcombe House, in Wroxall. The next time I ran past it I knew a lot more about it, thanks to Edward.

Did he have a special feeling when he made his first visit to Osborne House, the former home of Queen Victoria?

"I'm sure I should have done but I didn't. It's a wonderful place but has been empty for too long. It's not been lived in. That's the first thing that struck me."

As we were leaving Petworth House we came out the same time as Edward and his detective. We were just chatting together as he headed towards the rather posh chauffeured royal car. Luckily, my diesel Mondeo was hidden around the corner.

I met him again in 2016 when, as the Earl of Wessex, he made a visit to Isle of Wight Radio. Obviously, he didn't remember choosing that Frank Ifield record but it brought laughter all around.

CHAPTER 20

Arthur Worsley

THANKS TO SUMMER SHOW PRODUCER John Redgrave I was able to meet so many of my particular favourite light entertainment stars. He brought them to Sandown Pavilion and many are featured in this book. I have always loved ventriloquists and this all began by listening to Peter Brough and Archie Andrews in the hit radio series Educating Archie. When I was sat in the tin bath in front of the fire, I was too young to realise a vent on the radio was not particularly clever. A few years on when I saw Arthur Worsley on Sunday Night At The London Palladium I realised I was watching the best in the business – not forgetting 'Charlie Brown', of course.

Imagine my excitement when I had the pre-Christmas tip off that he'd been booked for the following summer of 1978, as one of the stars of Holiday Spectacular, alongside John Boulter and, in the peak weeks, Mike and Bernie Winters.

I was invited to afternoon tea with Arthur and his wife Audrey. They were renting a flat in Seaview, where MPs and Penelope Keith have had summer homes. Famous people were rarely troubled in this picturesque seaside village but on one occasion Arthur walked 200 yards to buy a pint of milk and nine people went out of their way to say hello. Initially, it was purely my work, as a showbiz columnist, to interview the master vent. We became great friends and met socially and were invited to bring our four-year-old son to tea, and later they came back to us. We kept in regular contact with Arthur and Audrey for many years.

Arthur was such a lovely modest star and during our first chat he casually told me he had appeared with Elvis Presley on the world famous Ed Sullivan American television show. I was astounded and had been an Elvis fan since the first time I ever heard him. He remembered Elvis being a particularly "nice young man" and it was the king of rock 'n' roll's first ever appearance on the show.

"We chatted away backstage and all around the theatre were thousands of screaming girls literally pulling their hair out," said Arthur, who appeared several times on the Ed Sullivan Show, alongside stars like Esther Williams and Jimmy Durante. An incredible 78 million people watched the show.

Arthur's reputation, as the best ventriloquist in the world, took him on several tours to Germany, South Africa, Australia, America and New Zealand.

The advent of television light entertainment shows suddenly found out some inferior ventriloquists. In the theatres very few beyond the first six rows could ever tell if their lips were moving or not. With the intimacy of television cameras it was altogether different.

In Britain, Arthur had 11 seasons at the London Palladium and topped the bill over stars like Morecambe and Wise, Harry Secombe and Benny Hill.

During that summer of '78, I was made up in drag by Burden and Moran for a newspaper story. They took 'the new me' into Arthur's dressing room to meet him. He said: "Have me met before? I seem to know your face from somewhere." In fact, he had no idea it was me. It was a priceless moment.

I also loved the occasion Sean met Charlie Brown for the first time, which is pictured on the left.

CHAPTER 21

Sheridan Smith

THE SCAPEGOAT is one of my favourite films. I've watched it at least a dozen times. I was invited to the Isle of Wight premiere in the late summer of 2012. The movie, also seen on television, was produced by two local friends, Dominic Minghella and Sarah Beardsall. I was thrilled to be asked to chair the Q & A after the screening. Among the guests on the panel was the wonderful Sheridan Smith, one of the stars of the movie.

Once I realised she was going to be on the panel I immediately contacted her agent to see if there was any chance of an interview. They asked how long did I want and seemed horrified when I said around 30 minutes. I was told, rather bluntly, she might give me about 10 minutes but no more.

On the day of the screening I thought I would bide my time and then make a move, if the opportunity arose. The movie got a great reception and the Q & A was very successful and much appreciated by the audience. Sheridan was very friendly and after the event she came over to thank me. Here was my big chance. I asked if I could interview her the following morning before she went back to London. She invited me to her hotel, the Royal, in Ventnor, to have breakfast with her and do an interview.

Over coffee and toast Sheridan asked how long would I would want for the interview. When I asked for 30 minutes she replied I could have as long as I wanted. In the end, I got a little more and she was in brilliant form. After our chat she talked about getting a taxi to drive her and her long-term friend and PA, Edwina Northcott, back to the ferry, which was around ten miles away. I volunteered to drive them and this gesture was hastily accepted.

Sheridan told me there was no rush and we had more coffee and a walk around the garden, which overlooked the sea. Then there were pictures taken outside the entrance to the posh hotel. The hotel manager, who had been so helpful to me, joined us and on hearing I was to drive them to the ferry he suddenly pulled rank and told them he would take them in his posh 4x4. I'm sure they would have liked my orange Ford Focus just as much. The astute manager was probably eyeing his business interests with the possibility of a return visit for Miss Smith.

I found Sheridan such great company. She was delightfully modest and pure fun to be with. In fact, she was just like any ordinary lady you could meet in the street. No airs and graces whatsoever. During the interview she revealed her early beginnings and how she sang with her mother and father, who were a country music duo.

She also hinted that she was playing Ronnie Biggs' wife in a new series called *Mrs Biggs*, much of which was filmed in Australia. This went on to be such a huge hit and paved the way for *Cilla*, *The C Word*, *The 7.39*, *The Moorside*, *Funny Girl* and numerous other successes.

I was disappointed the national media gave her such a rough time during her health problems while appearing in the West End production of *Funny Girl*. I watch whatever Sheridan Smith does. If she's in it, I know it's bound to be good. *Cilla* was the perfect example. In that one she got the whole country talking.

CHAPTER 22

Roy Castle

WHEN I DO CHARITY TALKS about my 44 years as an interviewer, I am often asked who have been some of my favourite people. Roy Castle is always among my answers. It was a real pleasure to have known him and he was such a credit to his business. Nothing was too much trouble and he always found time for an interview and was genuinely pleased to see you.

I first met Roy back in 1977 when he was booked to appear at the Ponda Rosa cabaret club, near Ryde. It was a sell-out and everyone just marvelled at his array of talents. Roy could do anything. He was so successful and was later booked for five consecutive nights in the pre-Christmas build up and they were all sold out. I always remember him lying on his back and playing *The Flight Of The Bumblebee* to a standing ovation.

During that first interview he revealed that he wanted to be a Frank Sinatra-type crooner, but a guy called Elvis Presley came along and changed all that. *Heartbreak Hotel* brought no tears for Roy. He merely changed direction to include comedy, impressions, trumpet playing and singing. Very astute – and it paid off.

Roy could make everything look easy. He danced his way into West End musicals, won a generation of young fans from his legendary *Record Breakers* days and even had the odd hit record. Some of his televised comedy sketches with Jimmy James still delight people on YouTube and various nostalgia channels.

I initially started broadcasting on hospital radio before moving on to a 26-year chat show on commercial radio. One Christmas Eve we did a live link with a Bristol

Roy Castle (left) with Bob Muir

hospital radio network. I had pre-recorded a piece with Roy for transmission on that special night. With his admirable Christian beliefs he was the perfect choice. Things went well until Bristol asked to speak to him live on air. How could I get out of this one? I told them he had left to catch the last ferry back to Portsmouth. Well, they did stop running earlier than usual on Christmas Eve.

On his very first visit to the Ponda Rosa, Roy was reunited with an old pal called Bob Muir, who had moved to the Isle of Wight. They had appeared together many years earlier in a summer show at Cleveleys, in Lancashire.

Over the years I interviewed Roy on numerous occasions but our last ever meeting stills tugs on my emotions. The night was February 28, 1993 at the Kings Theatre, Southsea. He was topping the bill in a special show to raise money for the Wessex Cancer Care. His co-stars included Julie Rogers and Craig Douglas. It had been sold out for weeks and a lot of money was raised.

I can remember going back to Roy's hotel with the other stars to do a few interviews and to celebrate the success of a wonderful evening. Roy and I were in the lift and heading to his room for an interview. He was in an ebullient mood. A few days earlier he had been given the all clear from his cancer. It was such a joyous occasion.

There was not a happy ending. The lovely Roy was not spared from that dreadful disease. The way he tackled his farewell tour, when clearly not well, brought tears to millions of his fans. There will never be another Roy Castle.

CHAPTER 23

Victoria Wood

ONE SATURDAY MORNING in August 2000 I had a surprise phone call from one of Britain's greatest theatrical agents, Richard Stone, who lived about ten miles from me. We had become friends a year or two before that. I'll never forget his exciting opening words. "Can you get over to my house within the next hour because Victoria Wood is here with me and is very happy to talk to you?" Richard had kept a promise to me and I made it in time. Victoria and her son, Henry, had plans to visit the Robin Hill Country Park, but were happy to delay their trip for a few minutes.

While setting up my radio equipment I thought of a good idea – and it worked perfectly. I welcomed Richard back to my show and asked him how he had met Victoria Wood, who had written the foreword to his forthcoming book. He said: "Why don't you ask her, as she's sat next to me."

In fact when Victoria first met Richard Stone she was struggling to make a living, or, more likely, was not even making one.

"I had, supposedly, been working for three years but in honesty I was doing very little at all. I had a strange manager and an odd contract with another agency. I don't know why but I wrote to Roger Hancock, Tony Hancock's brother, who was more of a literary agent. He advised me to go and see Richard Stone, who was a very reputable agent."

This was in the spring of 1977 and Victoria stayed with Richard for 20 years.

"The first thing he asked me was 'have you got good legs because if you have I could use you in pantomimes?' I never did get that call for a pantomime."

Victoria had a few horrendous early gigs, like playing to 18 squaddies at the Catterick army camp. Actually, Richard had initially told her that if she didn't earn £10,000 in the first year he would let her go. She had no contract and never came near that sum for a few years.

Like many others, I first saw Victoria on *New Faces*, her major television break, and I had remembered it vividly, as she had done. The reason being, panelist Clifford Davis told her she would never work. She never ever met him again, but I bet he was embarrassed by her rise to great stardom, particularly when she twice sold out 14 nights in a row at the Royal Albert Hall. There were 5000 people at every one of the 28 nights. Then came the hugely successful *Victoria Wood As Seen On TV*.

Later on in her career, she wrote the brilliant television series *Dinner Ladies*, which peaked at an audience of over 15 million.

"It was really two years of solid hard work. We actually only did 16 episodes but writing them myself, co-producing and appearing in them was rather tough.

"I had left Richard's agency by that time but, as ever, he was the first person to ring me after the first episode. He always did that. I owe such a lot to him. He was such a gent and never went back on his word."

Richard told me he asked Victoria to pen the foreword to his book right in the middle of her writing the *Dinner Ladies* scripts. The very next day it was on his desk.

Victoria, sadly, one of several great stars who died in 2016, had been a regular visitor to Richard's Isle of Wight home at Seaview and he used to take her children on trips in his boat. She also had a long-term pal who lived a few miles away in Cowes, the gorgeous Celia Imrie. They worked together on so many occasions. I never knew that when Victoria moved up north, Celia drove the furniture van.

CHAPTER 24
Bobby Davro

IN MAY 1981 I BECAME FRIENDS with an unknown young impressionist who was playing an early summer season at Sandown. He often needed consoling after facing the early season oldies who just couldn't keep up with his brilliant quick-fire humour. Many of his clever routines, which included a great *University Challenge* skit, went straight over their heads. Then just 22, he was still finding his feet in the business and supporting bill-topper Dai Francis. During that show, I managed to get him his first ever write up in T*he Stage* newspaper and he was so chuffed.

Five years later he came back to the same theatre and drew 1200 people by his own star billing. I had predicted in my original 1981 show review that he would become a star.

Had the boy changed or had nationwide fame gone to his head? Since our last meeting there had been several stories in national newspapers and not all were complimentary.

As I walked into his dressing room any doubts I may have had were instantly wiped away. "Hello mate, how are you? Want to have a chat?" Then came a warm handshake.

Being a young miler who'd run in the All England School's Championships, I knew the name of Bobby's father, Bill Nankeville. He was a great runner and had influenced my schoolboy hero Roger Bannister. I reckon I could have beaten young Davro over a mile but certainly couldn't imitate Prince Charles or Bamber Gascoyne.

During those five years between our interviews, Bobby had really taken off via hit shows like *Copy Cats* and his own series called *Davro On The Box*. These had all been set up via his sensational appearance on *Live From Her Majesty's*.

I loved the *Copy Cats* series and had interviewed virtually everyone in it. Imagine my delight when the TV T*imes* rang to ask if I would write a large two-page article on the show and its stars. The money offered was 20 times more than I got for my showbiz column in the local paper. I was so excited to open the TV T*imes* and see my huge spread – only to find my name spelt wrong.

Back to Bobby and his impressions. He did a pretty mean Alex Higgins. Had he ever met the snooker legend?

"No I've never actually met him but one or two snooker players tell me he is not too enamoured with my impression. Actually, he's a great sporting hero of mine. That's why I do it, so he should be flattered."

In 1986 I left Bobby at the stage door where he faced a huge queue of fans wanting autographs and photos. Five years earlier he'd walked thought the same stage door and no-one recognised him. That's the miracle of showbusiness and young Davro deserved everything he had achieved.

I did feel so sorry for him when the press invaded his private life and gave him a hard time. I was not surprised when he told me most of it was completely untrue. I didn't want to talk about it. That's never been my style.

In 2015 I had an interview all lined up with Bobby when he visited the Gurnard Pines Holiday Park. Sadly, due to travel problems, he missed his scheduled ferry and arrived too late for a chat. I hope I get another opportunity.

Bobby is pictured at Sandown Pavilion in 1981.

CHAPTER 25

Rick Wakeman

THE FIRST TIME I ever saw Rick Wakeman he came flying past me and I had a job to catch him up. There was not a stage or keyboard anywhere in sight – just the football pitch of the Wessex League team Cowes Sports. This particular game was a charity match between the local team and the Showbiz XI. As I reported on their matches and had a showbiz column in the local paper, I was asked to make a guest appearance and found myself trying to mark a guy who had sold well over 70 million albums. I had seen the back of a Showbiz XI player earlier and he had the Rick Wakeman Tour logo on his t-shirt. I wrongly assumed he was probably a roadie.

It was a year or two before I officially met Rick. This time it was backstage at Sandown Pavilion and we just gelled from the very first minute. Well Rick is that kind of guy.

During that first meeting in 1988 he told me a remarkable story. On Friday, January 18, 1974, Rick received a writ from Express Dairies for not paying his milk bill. That night his future was in the balance on stage at the Royal Festival Hall. But *Journey To The Centre Of The Earth* was so successful it could have kept the audience in milk for the rest of their lives.

"It really started everything off for me as a solo performer. Nobody believed we could do it and even the record company didn't really want it. I was mortgaged up to the hilt to fund it and couldn't pay a single bill at the time. If Journey hadn't worked, I would have been finished, both careerwise and financially."

There were almost 300 on stage that night. Augmenting Rick and his keyboards were the London Symphony Orchestra, the English Chamber Choir and his own band and singers. David Hemmings compèred the mammoth production.

Rick is so witty and has a story for any occasion. Over the years we have met many times and on one memorable Sunday he bowled into the Isle of Wight Radio studio to appear live on my chat show. That was a gamble in itself but he was on his best behaviour. There was a reason. He had his current wife with him. From memory, I think it was his third. I love Rick but that day I definitely looked at his wife much more. Well, it was supermodel Nina Carter, who, I think, even managed to tame him for a while.

Suddenly a wee bit later he became the darling of the retired set, following his appearances on *Countdown*. Then so many other series followed, like *Grumpy Old Men*. He's had his own radio and TV shows and has a gift for taking everything in his stride. When he lived in the Isle of Man he produced an album for his neighbour, Norman Wisdom.

I last met Rick at a Premiere Inn on the Isle of Wight. He was suddenly in the news for his piano tribute to David Bowie, who had just tragically died. Millions had gone on to the internet to listen to his new version of *Life On Mars*. He'd played on the original session. Rick's 2017 album that followed made the Top Ten.

Many years earlier my wife, who was a huge fan of piano players, had told Rick, before a concert, that she was also a great fan of Richard Clayderman. I'll never forget his instant reply: "Heather, I'm sorry we don't play for insomniacs."

CHAPTER 26

Roy Hudd

I FIRST MET ROY HUDD back in the early summer of 1976. He was as friendly as I expected and his showbiz knowledge is second to none. I also caught up with him again later that year when he was starring in summer season at Paignton. That was a sort of busman's holiday for me, as I also interviewed Moira Anderson at the nearby Princess Theatre in Torquay.

The following year Roy came to star in a Sunday Concert at Shanklin Theatre. It proved a unique experience for him. He was such an expert on the old stars of music hall and variety, but had never seen Barney Powell perform. Barney, who had come to the Isle of Wight for summer seasons with Tommy Trinder, back in the '30s, had a famous local emporium just down the hill from the theatre. He was a support act on Roy's show. We both stood in the wings watching Barney and Roy became quite emotional. In his younger days, Barney had appeared at the Windmill and had been given a pair of dancing shoes by an unknown Bruce Forsyth. They probably didn't help Barney that much – as he played the xylophone.

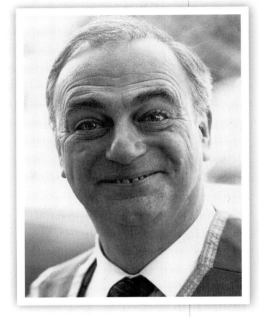

Roy invited me to come to the Pavilion Theatre, Bournemouth, to see him play Fagin in *Oliver*. Amazingly, he had never seen the stage show or the movie so he created his own Fagin and was quite superb.

"One of my toughest problems at the moment is to step out of character to play Sunday Concerts. I sometimes forget myself and talk like Fagin," said Roy.

Our paths were to cross many times in the following years. I remember him coming to Ryde to support a special luncheon in aid of the Water Rats. Joining Roy were Danny La Rue and Norman Wisdom, who both feature in this book.

One of the most popular records on my Sunday lunchtime chat show was *Peeping Tom*, sung by Roy. It was a very funny take-off of the Singing Postman.

On a whim, in the 90s, I contacted Roy to see if I could come up to Broadcasting House to see a live recording of his hit show *The News Hudd Lines*. My good friend Vic Farrow, a very successful show promoter on the Isle of Wight, joined me. It was a memorable occasion. I interviewed Roy after the recording and casually asked how I could get an interview with one of his co-stars, June Whitfield. He just told me to send the letter to him and he would do the rest. In less than a month, I was in her house in Wimbledon. She even drove me back to the station in her great old car.

A few years later Roy was coming back to Shanklin Theatre to perform one of his own unique shows, with his wife Debbie, and I arranged to go to London to pre-record an interview. Roy, as generous as ever, came down from Suffolk just to talk to me. He chose the venue – and it was perfect. We met at the Water Rats headquarters in King's Cross. Roy also found time to show me around their fascinating museum.

Roy is now also an established straight actor and has been seen in *Coronation Street*, as undertaker Archie Shuttleworth, *Common As Muck*, *Missing* and *Broadchurch*. I had to tease him about playing Harold Atterbow, an organist who was simply a dirty old man. There was one amazing scene in *Lipstick On Your Collar* when he was in his van with a beautiful young blonde. All us guys were so envious.

"That scene was a bit scary but I kept getting it wrong so I could do it again," said Roy, with a glint in his eye.

CHAPTER 27

Sarah Douglas

I HAD A PHONE CALL on a summer's day in 1977 from a freelance photographer who lived just a few hundred yards from me. Apparently, he'd got a scoop for us in the nearby village of Wroxall and would be calling for me in a few minutes. It was quite a surprise, too. One of Britain's fastest-rising, young movie starlets, Sarah Douglas, was attending a private children's birthday party. It certainly was a great story, as her latest movie, *The People That Time Forgot*, had been showing in local cinemas.

When we arrived, my photographer led the way and we were quickly inside the house. Despite our intrusion we were welcomed and pictures were taken and Sarah willingly gave me an impromptu interview. I was relieved because it had not been my normal kind of interview approach.

I quickly realised that Sarah had a hard professional attitude towards her screen career and I was left in little doubt that she was set to go right to the top. So a couple of years later I was not surprised to see her turn up as Ursa in the *Superman* movies followed by Queen Taramis in *Conan The Destroyer*. In the '80s she spent two years in the American soap *Falcon Crest*.

Over a coffee, Sarah talked fondly of her early life in Stratford and of joining the National Youth Theatre, at the age of 14. With her fellow young actors she toured the continent and made a few television appearances.

Sarah's family were far from happy with her infatuation for the stage and for a while she went to France as an English governess, but in the end her dreams came true and she ended up at drama school. Early on in her career she played small parts in movies like *The Final Programme*, *The Last Days Of Man On Earth* and *Dracula*. The latter starred Jack Palance and Simon Ward. On television she was a regular in hit series which included *Bergerac* and *The Professionals*.

Her name was up in lights in a West End show but not for too long. Sarah told me: "It opened and suddenly closed after a week. My family saw the first night and stayed for the last."

Had her lack of repertory experience ever been a problem? "It might have been some kind of hindrance. Two years ago I did try and get into rep and got the usual auditions. I had a long list of movie and TV credits but they said I had no rep experience. When I asked for small parts they said I had too many past credits. It was a vicious circle, so I went back to television. It was far more lucrative. Now that I've had three big movies in a row, £50 a week in rep is a difficult choice to make."

The People That Time Forgot was shot in the Canary Islands where on set she got her fair share of bumps and bruises. The other stars were Doug McClure, Patrick Wayne, the son of John Wayne, Thorley Walters and Dana Gillespie. Prior to this she had played the lead in the movie *The Brute*.

Her four-day private break on the Isle of Wight came after 17 weeks of filming on *Superman* and she was due to go back to it. She revealed very little about it other than confirming Gene Hackman and Marlon Brando were in it. It was certainly more exciting than an English repertory season.

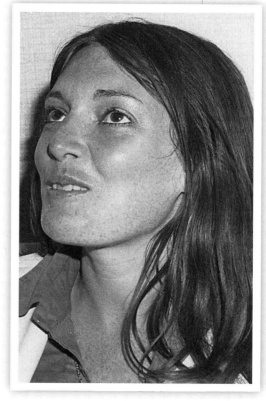

CHAPTER 28

Stephane Grappelli

FRIDAY DECEMBER 5, 1975, was a night I will never forget. I left home early in the evening to head for Sandown Pavilion to see the legendary French violinist Stephane Grappelli. I loved the concert and was so thrilled when he gave me a short interview. I could not believe his stamina. He'd had to stand all the way down on the train from Waterloo to Portsmouth and then for over two hours on stage. At least he sat down when I interviewed him.

The show itself was simply amazing and three top British jazz musicians led by guitarist Diz Disley formed the brilliant trio that accompanied him. Also on stage was another guitar legend, Ike Isaacs, and bass genius Phil Bates. After casually strolling on to join the other musicians Stephane proceeded to captivate everyone including his own stage musicians. My particular favourites were *Summertime, Tea For Two* and *I Only Have Eyes For You.*

As I was leaving the seafront theatre, Stephane, who had left some minutes earlier, came rushing back looking very distressed. He saw me and rushed over. Apparently, he'd tried to enter his hotel just a few yards up the road but was barred by a huge and vicious dog.

"This dog will not let me in and I am too frightened to try and enter. My hands are insured for £10,000 and I can't take the risk of being bitten. Can you help me please?"

Finding him another hotel on a cold and late early December night in an out-of-season resort was not going to be easy. I bundled him into my car and drove him six miles to Ryde where I knew there was a business hotel that might just have a room. Imagine my relief when they were able to help. Then he told me he had not eaten and asked if there was a late night restaurant nearby. I knew of a Chinese restaurant just 200 yards up the road and he asked me to join him, as I had been so kind.

I almost felt like asking Stephane to ring my wife to check whether I would be locked out. I found the courage and rang her from the hotel. I can't remember what she said – but it wasn't have a lovely time. Thankfully, there was no lock out and I took her to Stephane's next concert on the Isle of Wight and she became an instant fan of his music.

Thanks to a wild dog, six miles up the coast, I enjoyed an unexpected late night supper with Stephane Grappelli and just sat there transfixed by his wartime stories and memories of his days in the Quintet Of The French Hot Club with Django Reinhardt.

I also took a vinyl album with me for Stephane to sign. It was the recording he'd made with Yehudi Menuhin. It may have seemed an unlikely combination but their diverse styles worked so beautifully together.

"I was pleased and honoured to play with the great violinist. We had a good time together and he is a man with a lot of spirit," added Stephane.

CHAPTER 29

Brian Conley

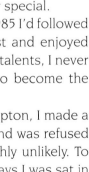

SUNDAY AUGUST 4, 1985, was another memorable day. The new star comedian Jimmy Cricket did two concerts on Sandown Pier and close on 2000 people saw the shows. Two years earlier he'd played a summer season there just before he'd became a household name. I love surprises and I had one when one of his supporting company got me so excited that I raced to his dressing room in the interval to have a quick chat. I'd never heard of the guy. His name was Brian Conley.

I was invited into his dressing room and duly introduced myself. Brian could barely believe it. "No one ever comes to interview a supporting act," he said, with some amazement. I can still vividly remember telling him he was destined to become a huge star. I'm not so sure he believed it. On that show he did some gags, sang a bit and even found time for some fire eating.

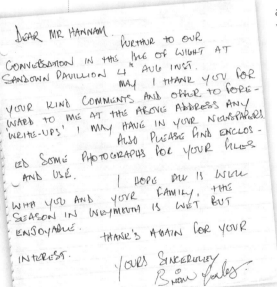

Imagine my surprise a few days later when I received a letter from Brian. He was in a summer season show in Weymouth and wanted to say how grateful he was. I still have it. Nearly 30 years later he came on to my radio chat show and actually told listeners the story behind our first meeting. That was a special day, too. Brian's lovely wife, Anne-Marie, made her radio debut on that show. It shook him as he expected her to say no.

A year or two after our first meeting in Sandown, I noticed Brian was starring with The Grumbleweeds in a Great Yarmouth summer season. We were on a family holiday close by. We waited outside the theatre to see him arrive and he had quite a surprise. He quickly sorted out tickets for the four of us and we all went backstage after the show. There were photographs taken and it made that holiday rather special.

Following the Sunday Concert in 1985 I'd followed Brian's career with particular interest and enjoyed his rise to real stardom. Despite being so appreciative of his obvious talents, I never expected to marvel at his performance as Al Jolson or see him rise to become the hottest pantomime star in Britain.

During one of his many successes at the Mayflower Theatre, Southampton, I made a request to record a face-to-face interview with him for my radio show and was refused by the PR company. Had stardom changed him? I thought this was highly unlikely. To make sure, I posted a personal letter to him at the theatre. Within two days I was sat in his dressing room with my recorder running.

"Nobody told me it was you. I was just told it was Isle of Wight Radio. You are welcome any time."

On another not so memorable occasion, I was sat with him at the Chichester Festival Theatre. I think he was starring in *The Music Man*. It all started brilliantly, but then my recorder gave up the ghost and I had to be content with about 10 minutes.

It's a strange world. In that Great Yarmouth summer season my young daughter, Caroline, had some pictures taken backstage with Brian, who was one of her favourites. She could never have anticipated that one day she would be the head of wardrobe in the West End production of *Hairspray*, which starred Brian Conley.

CHAPTER 30

Ted Rogers

MILLIONS KNEW TED ROGERS as the host of the number one television show *3-2-1*, with Dusty Bin and co. This brought Ted national fame but it was his double life as a slick stand-up comedian that brought him world fame. Huge stars like Bing Crosby, Perry Como and Andy Williams wanted him to support them on tours in Britain and America. They loved his topical gags.

Long before I got to know Ted Rogers I saw him in a series of Sunday Concerts he did with Joan Regan and still have the autographed programme. When I eventually got to meet him it was all down to a guy who grew up on the Isle of Wight, Wally Malston, who was previously mentioned in the chapter on Bob Monkhouse. He became Ted's resident scriptwriter and travelled with him the whole time, writing topical gags as they went along. Sometimes they were written just an hour or two before Ted went on stage.

On one occasion I was so privileged to be given an interview opportunity by Ted on a particular weekend when he'd flatly refused to talk to any journalists, including several

from national newspapers. This was due to us being personal friends and he knew I was not interested in private lives. I did not abuse this trust and was not interested in making a few quick bucks by stringing things on to the mass media.

I was very embarrassed on one occasion when we met Ted for a private drink after a show. With such a famous face he was instantly recognised. It seemed a young guy, egged on my his mates, was dared to verbally insult him. Luckily, I am not a violent man – otherwise I might well have hit him. Ted handled it so well and we moved on.

Very few stars would provide their own babysitter but Ted did. I had a friend who ran the highly acclaimed Farringford Hotel at Freshwater, which was once the home of Lord Alfred Tennyson. He invited us to take Ted and his wife Marion to dinner at their wonderful hotel. It would be great publicity. Unfortunately, we could not get a babysitter, but Ted solved the problem. His in-laws were staying with him in the house he was renting for a summer season and he volunteered them for the job. On that occasion diners were visibly thrilled to see Ted on a nearby table.

Ted loved working with the world stars and Bing Crosby was his particular favourite and they also met socially. He was his support act on numerous occasions in both the West End and on Broadway. He was due to work with Bing in Australia, Japan and New Zealand but the legendary crooner died a month or two before.

He was a workaholic and for a while, during a season at the London Palladium, he would drive down to the Minehead Butlin's Holiday Centre, after the evening show, to do a midnight cabaret.

Ted always tried to get home every night, after a performance. When he toured with Shirley Bassey she said to him, on one occasion: "Darling, where do you go after the show every night?" She just could not believe he went home – and he'd probably taken the children to school before Miss Bassey had got up.

I remember one night he brought the family to Warner's, Bembridge Coast Hotel, where he was appearing in cabaret. They had a chalet but after the show he picked his son up, who was fast asleep, and laid him in the back of the car en route to the last ferry of the evening.

I owe a huge debt to Ted because he introduced me to Bruce Forsyth. More of that later.

CHAPTER 31
Cathy Tyson

I LOVED WATCHING Cathy Tyson in her movie debut, when she played alongside Michael Caine and Bob Hoskins, and not forgetting the white rabbit, in *Mona Lisa*. It was a stunning performance and then I never missed an episode of *Band Of Gold*. I did try for an interview but got nowhere. In this business you must never give up. It took me 18 years to get Gene Pitney but I would have waited even longer for Miss Tyson. Luckily, I didn't have to.

At that time Southampton's Nuffield Theatre was presenting big names in their productions. I could hardly believe it when a press release arrived for a play called *The Shagaround*, which starred, among others, Cathy Tyson. My email request for an interview was off within five minutes.

It was quickly confirmed. The day arrived and I was happy for an early morning visit to Sainsbury's to pave the wave to nip over to Southampton for the interview. On the way home from the shopping trip I had a call on my mobile, which my wife answered. I sensed a wind-up when she told me Cathy had been held up in traffic and would not be at the theatre in time to be interviewed. Was this purely a big tease? No, in fact it was true. Another date was set but a call came in again on the very day to say she was ill and would not be well enough to be interviewed. Heather couldn't resist saying: "I don't think she wants to see you."

The next suggested date was a Bank Holiday. Southampton was quite quiet but I managed to get a bus to the Nuffield. There was not a single person around in the theatre foyer and I feared the worst. Suddenly, in through a door walked Cathy, who immediately said: "You must be John." I was so relieved.

Cathy, whose great aunt was a nun, was brought up in Liverpool by her mother, Margaret, who was a single parent. Life was not easy but she told me of her vivid memories of massive crowds of people in the city. At primary school she was very shy and hated drama. This was to change at secondary school and later at the local Everyman Theatre, when she appeared in a production called *In The City*, in which she was seen as an old lady who fed the ducks. This was a hint of what was to come, as she had an early chance to talk to an audience.

Success at the Everyman eventually led her to the Royal Shakespeare Company at Stratford, which was something of a culture shock.

"It seemed I was in the middle class area that I'd rebelled against. At first, I was reluctant to embrace it with open arms. I'd come from Liverpool and still had lots of feelings about being black amidst a majority of white people and of being very defensive. I was only 18 and had so many feelings going on, as well as having so many things to learn," said Cathy.

In fact, she worked so hard with rehearsals, playing parts and reading scripts that she missed much of the social life that 18-year-olds enjoy. I was delighted to hear that she'd made up for it since then.

"I was so surprised to get *Mona Lisa*. I was only 20 and it was my first movie. I was so sure I hadn't got the part and even left the script behind. This proved such a learning curve for me."

Before I left, I had to mention that my thoughts on chicken farmers had changed since I saw *Band Of Gold*. Nylons and Marigold gloves seemed much more fun!

CHAPTER 32

Charlton Heston

IT WAS THE SUMMER OF 1998 when Charlton Heston came to England to attend his beloved Wimbledon tennis tournament. By sheer coincidence, his wife Lydia had a joint photographic exhibition on the Isle of Wight with Koo Stark and I managed to interview them both. It was rumoured Charlton might find time to attend the exhibition at Dimbola Lodge, in Freshwater Bay, the former home of world-famous photographer Margaret Cameron. Amazingly, it happened and he arrived in a very special vintage car a little later than expected.

I was one of the local media who was invited to the event. I suddenly realised there would be no chance of a quick one-to-one chat with the star of movies like *Ben Hur* and *The Big Country*. A quick press conference was arranged and the news hounds were allowed one question, if they were lucky. I decided to remain in the background as an interested bystander. One quick fire question was hardly the thing for a radio chat show. At least I'd seen one of my all-time Hollywood idols on my own doorstep.

A few weeks after all the excitement had died down I had a phone call from a talented local photographer called Peter White, a good friend of mine. He asked me an unexpected question: "How did your interview go with Chuck Heston?" I explained my predicament and that it was not really convenient due to time restraints. Peter was disappointed and told me he was a personal friend of Charlton and Lydia and all might not be lost.

A few months later Peter got back in-touch and said Charlton and Lydia were coming to London to undertake a two hander play called *Love Letters*, at the Theatre Royal, Haymarket, and that he was certain he could get me an interview. The call came in early July and Peter told me to ring the Athenaeum Hotel, in Piccadilly, to speak to Charlton and that he was willing to do an interview.

I rang the hotel and was immediately put through to their room and Charlton answered the call. He was expecting me to ring and all the arrangements were quickly tied up.

The day came and it was a scorcher and I arrived at the Athenaeum rather hot, carrying my equipment which included a double microphone stand. A doorman quickly grabbed my gear and took me into the lounge and looked after it while I freshened up.

I was invited to join Charlton and Lydia at their table in the dining room and quickly realised what life must be like for a Hollywood icon. You could sense all eyes were focused on his table – and it must have been like that wherever he went.

"John, have you eaten?" asked Charlton, who then insisted I call him Chuck. Actually I hadn't and on hearing that, Chuck quickly summoned a waiter to our table. I was offered smoked salmon sandwiches. After a few minutes they had not arrived and Chuck flicked his fingers to a waiter and they soon appeared.

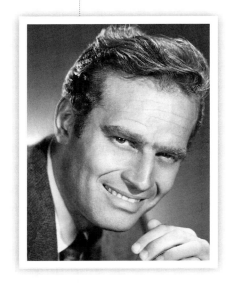

Whilst he went to the cloakroom, I quietly asked Lydia, whom I'd found so charming at our Dimbola interview the year before, how long would be acceptable. I wanted an hour but suggested 45 minutes. When Chuck came back she mentioned the 45 minutes and he replied: "I've never done an interview that long in my life. We'll see how it goes."

The hotel found us a quiet room. I was so glad Lydia was there as Chuck was showing slight early signs of memory problems and she knew all the answers and prompted him on a handful of occasions. These were superbly voiced so they could be easily edited out. Oh, and by the way – I got over an hour's conversation with him.

CHAPTER 33

Danny La Rue

"LEAVE IT TO ME MATE – but don't go to bed!" These were the words a locally-based entertainer called Tony Scott whispered to me at the end of a Danny La Rue Sunday Concert.

Tony was my go-between for a possible interview with his long time pal Danny La Rue. He was so keen to counteract my obvious disappointment of the previous year when I got nowhere near to chatting to the master of female impersonation. Would I be lucky this time around?

With my wife fast asleep in bed the phone rang at 1.25am. Luckily, it did not wake her as I was still downstairs and had grabbed the receiver straight away. This was long before all those cold calls from India to tell me my computer has a problem. It was welcome news. Danny would see me at 10.15am, later that morning. Scotty had achieved his promise.

It was the beginning of a long friendship with Danny. We met on numerous occasions and he was always such genial company. I would sometimes ring him up at his Southampton home for a quick chat. Heather was a huge Danny La Rue fan and she came on one or two interviews just to marvel at his wardrobe.

Danny was a true showbiz legend and he always found time to talk. On the last occasion we met, when his huge shows had been scaled down, he revealed the story of how he became virtually bankrupt overnight. He fought back from this and rebuilt his career with great personal satisfaction.

During our first meeting, back in 1985, Danny was working 48 weeks of the year and spent most of his time in coaches, cars, planes and hotels. At times, he occasionally pondered for a return to the simplicity of his early life. He admitted his success was wonderful and fully appreciated. It also meant thousands of interviews all over the world but he preferred this to nobody asking.

"Life is destiny," explained Danny. "Doris Stokes always rings me up because she thinks I'm psychic. I'm not really but just have a great feeling for people and the world."

Danny was the prime reason female impersonation became more legitimate and upmarket. Its once tarnished image was forgotten via his spectacular West End seasons and national tours. It was so hard to even buy a ticket to see a Danny La Rue show. On the road he travelled with 29 people and all of them had to be paid.

"I suppose I could travel with just 10 and people would still come and see me but not go home satisfied. I give the best I can give, in the dresses and in fact everything."

There will never be another Danny La Rue. He appeared in over 30 Royal shows, had seven major West End shows and appeared 16 times on *The Good Old Days*. He worked to millions and was a supreme professional.

By the time we had our last conversation, for my radio chat show, he had become disillusioned with his business and some of the people who were far less professional than him and many of his contemporaries. The crude shows that had begun to creep in were a major disappointment to him. Danny hated filth and on one tour he reprimanded his support comic for going too far.

Danny was unique and loved by sophisticated ladies and taxi drivers. He loved the London cabbies who always greeted him with "Whatcha mate." Nice one Dan!

CHAPTER 34
Deryck Guyler

FROM AN EARLY AGE, both Sean and Caroline quickly got used to meeting famous stars and people like Ted Rogers became 'uncle Ted' and Craig Douglas 'uncle Craig.' They also looked on Deryck Guyler as a friendly uncle due, to his close friendship with Billy Whittaker and Mimi Law, personal friends of ours.

One Saturday night in 1990 I took my two young people on a trip to pick up Deryck en route to his live appearance on my radio show. It all went smoothly until the return journey through torrential rain. We had to avoid floating manhole covers and had important passengers, which included several famous names. On board were Frisby Dyke, from *ITMA*, Corky the policeman seen in the Eric Sykes TV series, Potter the caretaker from *Please Sir!* and Number One from the hit radio series *The Men From The Ministry*. Deryck readily admitted to be all of them.

He was one of those people you could listen to for hours with such a soothing voice and a relaxed style of recalling wonderful stories. He'd worked with a few legends, too. There were names like Tony Hancock, Eric Barker, Dick Emery, Harry Worth and Tommy Handley.

Deryck actually got into comedy by accident. He was asked to join the cast of the biggest show on the radio, *ITMA*. It was wartime and millions listened every Thursday night.

He told me: "They preferred to use straight actors, which was how I got into the series. I was invalided out of action during the war and had joined the BBC Repertory Company and made 800 programmes."

Suddenly he became famous as the voice behind some of the show's most popular characters, namely Frisby Dyke, Percy Palaver and Sir Short Supply.

For a while after the war he appeared in 13 different radio shows every week. On one memorable day he did four live shows. Shrewdly, he was never really typecast due to him being so adaptable.

Deryck was a radio star who relished the chance to join the burgeoning television industry. In 1968 he was signed for *Please Sir!* and appeared in 58 episodes as Potter. That series was sold to virtually every country.

"I was in Australia on one occasion during a tour with Eric Sykes and Hattie Jacques and I was out for a walk and saw a huge lorry backing out of a street. The driver stopped reversing and shouted. 'How are you Potter? Got plenty of work on?' That was 12,000 miles from home," reflected Deryck.

He spent 20 years working on television with Eric, Hattie and Richard Wattis and was flattered to be called Corky when walking down any street in Great Britain and beyond.

Deryck was always grateful for an unexpected phone call. He was asked on a Saturday night if he could take over the role of Number One from Wilfred Hyde-White in the radio series *The Men From The Ministry*. It was for the following day. White had signed a Hollywood contract and would not be returning to the hit series. That led to 11 year's work.

He was also a highly acclaimed washboard player and this reached a peak when he was one of an all-star band seen by 20 million on *Children In Need*.

One of his less enjoyable moments was when he sold his collection of 1600 jazz records, all on 78s. He closed his eyes as they were taken away. I think his delightful wife Paddy might have breathed a sigh of relief.

I know we breathed a sigh of relief when we eventually got home after leaving Deryck on that stormy 1990 Saturday night.

CHAPTER 35

Felix Bowness

Back in 1977 I was walking by the Winter Gardens in Ventnor when I spotted a familiar face in the telephone box. I waited some time before he came out and he then apologised for being so long. He seemed surprised when I told him I didn't want to use the phone, I just wanted to meet him. That was my first ever encounter with Felix Bowness – and it was far from the last.

It was 11 years later when he made me stand up in front of over 2000 people at the London Palladium. More of that later.

Felix had made the Isle of Wight his second home. Following early appearances in Ventnor, a little later he had six summers seasons on Sandown Pier. The impresario of that time, Don Moody, was a great admirer of Felix. So much so that eventually Don's widow left the family home to Felix and his wife. Then my home phone never stopped ringing. Usually it was to ask if I could find him more work.

Even before his huge success as jockey Fred Quilley in *Hi-de-Hi*, Felix was a well known television face. He'd been seen in *Dad's Army*, *The Liver Birds*, *Porridge* and the shows of Cilla Black, Dick Emery and Les Dawson.

Felix was a very funny man and he had the knack of getting away with insulting his audience. In his giveaway shows he always picked on some poor unfortunate husband to take the mickey out of. The punters, particularly the wives, loved it. Tattoos have become so popular in recent years but back in the '70s Felix had so many words all over his hands and arms. They weren't actually tattoos – just his jokes written down in case he forgot any.

Felix also became so much in demand as a warm-up comedian for television shows. His job was to get the audience in high spirits before the cameras started rolling. All the top names wanted Felix on board and these included huge stars like Morecambe and Wise. Sometimes he was too funny and was asked to tone it down a bit because he was getting more laughs than the star was likely to get.

In 1988 it was our 25th wedding anniversary and Heather and I were invited for the weekend to the Fleet home of our friend Wally Malston, who was the script associate on *Sunday Night At The London Palladium* and he also wrote most of Jimmy Tarbuck's topical gags for the show.

We were in the audience for the October Sunday night show and in the afternoon were having tea with some of the stars and crew. Suddenly in walked Felix, who was the warm-up comic and he recognised me. "John, I might talk to you later," he hinted. It seemed somewhat ominous. "If I do, just say January 1."

Imagine the scene. There were 2,300 in a full Palladium laughing at the warm-up comedian. Then I suddenly wanted to run and hide. Felix told the audience: "There are two friends of mine in the front row of the circle. Will they both stand up." Heather pushed me up and suddenly I sensed trouble, as he told the audience it was my birthday. Jack Parnell and the boys in the orchestra started to play happy birthday and the audience sang along. Then Felix said: "It is your birthday isn't it?" When I replied: "No, it's January 1," it brought the house down. Then, within minutes, the cameras were rolling. That was one of over 6,000 TV warm-ups for Felix.

CHAPTER 36

Ian Bannen

WIVES OF WORKAHOLICS do have a lot to contend with. When I had a day job as a salesman and worked evenings and weekends as a freelance showbiz journalist and broadcaster, quite rightly, Heather sometimes put her foot down and, of course, she was right. Mind you, I had few complaints when she met some of her favourite stars, like Russ Conway, Frankie Vaughan, Nigel Havers and Frankie Howerd. Her support never

wavered and one day in 1996 she came home from her swimming session and was bursting with exciting news. She said: "I've got you an interview with Ian Bannen. I saw him at the pool today and asked him – and he said yes."

It was not a secret that Ian had a home in Ventnor but he was seldom around due to movie commitments. Thanks to Heather, I soon found myself in his house. I was a wee bit nervous, probably because of some of the screen roles I'd seen him in. Within minutes I was enjoying his hospitality and genial sense of humour.

I kept in touch with his lovely wife Marilyn and got an occasional postcard from them, from some exotic location where he was making a movie. In 1999 I tempted him into a live appearance on my radio chat show and he was in brilliant form. At that time, Ian was one of the hottest actors in the business. *Waking Ned*, a low budget movie made in just six weeks, had already grossed over 50 million dollars, and his fantastic performance had brought in so many offers.

He told me on that live radio interview how his life had changed. "Ten years ago when I first played an old man in *Hope And Glory* it started a new direction for me and I'm delighted about that."

During the three years between our interviews Ian had been the subject of a *This Is Your Life*. He was so thrilled when one of the surprise guests was Mel Gibson. Ian had appeared as a leper in Mel's acclaimed hit movie *Braveheart*.

Ian made over 70 major movies but never had any formal acting training. With no real experience he made his debut at the Gateway Theatre, Dublin. Within a few years he was playing in Shakespeare at Stratford with an equally unknown, Richard Burton. Over the years he also enjoyed a long friendship with Elizabeth Taylor, who also recorded a tribute for his *This Is Your Life*.

One of Ian's earliest theatrical memories was in a West End season of *A View From A Bridge*. Marilyn Monroe was in on opening night and went backstage to meet the cast. "I've never forgotten that night," added Ian.

Ian won BAFTA awards for his performances in *The Offence* and *Hope And Glory* and was nominated for an Oscar for *Flight Of The Phoenix*. His other film credits include *Ghandi*, *Gorky Park*, *The Hill*, *Too Late The Hero* and *Station Six Sahara*. Television fans loved his portrayal of Dr Cameron in the three '90s series of *Dr Finlay*.

At the age of 70, did he have any plans to retire?

"No, not until the Lord strikes me down," stressed Ian, who had recently won a BAFTA Lifetime Achievement Award.

Two of his movie projects were awaiting release. He'd already made *To Walk With Lions*, the follow up to *Born Free*, and *Best*, in which he played Sir Matt Busby.

Sadly, just a few months after our 1999 interview, Ian was killed in a car crash in Scotland. Thankfully, we can still enjoy his acting talents via some wonderful movies.

CHAPTER 37

Ken Dodd

BACK IN 1995 I'd given up any hope of Ken Dodd appearing on the Isle of Wight and a local friend, showbiz veteran Mimi Law, came up with the idea of us going to visit him. They had appeared together many times and her late husband, Billy Whittaker, had played dame to Ken on numerous occasions. In fact, Doddy had always asked for him to be in his pantomimes.

Ken was delighted at the thought of seeing Mimi again and we chose Hunstanton as the venue. So the three of us headed to Norfolk and after hold ups on the M25 we had problems finding any bed and breakfast guest houses. Eventually, not long before midnight, we found one just outside of Newmarket and we were given a warm welcome and a plate of sandwiches.

Ken Dodd with Heather and John

The next day we headed for Hunstanton and found another bed and breakfast gem. We were immediately given a key to the front door when they discovered we were going to a Ken Dodd concert. We had lunch and then found Doddy's hotel and were met by his partner Anne. He was upstairs running through the script for a new video but the promised interview would happen.

Ken breezed in and it was a moment to savour and within a few minutes he gave me an hour long interview. After a pot of tea with the three of us, Ken and Anne then headed for the theatre and said they would see us later. We did have one major problem. It was a sell-out and we had no tickets. We decided to go to the foyer of the theatre a few minutes before the show and hope something might happen – and it did. Anne came out and said we were Ken's guests and they had special tickets for us. It was such a relief.

The show began at 7.30pm and finished around 12.15am. In other words, a normal show for Ken Dodd. We had been asked to join him in his dressing room after the show. There were just a handful of us present and he started all over again and never stopped for an hour. The jokes and stories were different to those in the near five-hour show.

At 1.30, Heather, Mimi and I decided we ought to go back to the digs, as we had an early start in the morning to drive back to the Isle of Wight. It was hard to get away.

"Going so soon. The night is still young," insisted Ken. Then we left him to it.

On that Hunstanton interview he made me a promise, which was subsequently heard on air, that he would come to the Isle of Wight for a concert. He did keep his word and actually came 20 years later – and it was a full house. It was the longest show ever seen in Shanklin Theatre. The interval was just before 10pm and it finished the next day. What a performer and the caulkheads loved him. They are the name given to local residents. On that Hunstanton trip Ken had asked me if was a caulkhead. He'd obviously done his homework, too.

So I have such fond memories of interviewing Sir Ken Dodd, as he now is. A knighthood well deserved.

CHAPTER 38

Lynda Bellingham

I FIRST MET LYNDA in 1999 when she came to the Isle of Wight to film *Reach For The Moon*, the TV series which created such a lot of local interest. They recruited many Islanders as extras and, for a story, I spent a day as a window cleaner. I must have been on screen for at least two seconds – but I did get £80 expenses and two meals. By far the biggest thrill was having lunch with Lynda at Seaview's luxurious Priory Bay Hotel.

Caroline, worked on the production for work experience. The wardrobe personnel were so helpful to her and their knowledge helped her eventually end up as a West End costume supervisor, on shows like *Hairspray*, *The Last Tango* and *Driving Miss Daisy*. It also proved useful as she got dad interviews with a few of the star-studded cast, including Lynda Bellingham.

I'll never forget the day. We'd had a great interview in the hotel lounge and then headed for the restaurant for a light lunch. Midway through our meal, Lynda had a phone call from her son's school, where he was in a wee bit of trouble. A few years later she told me he'd actually been suspended at that time but had scraped through his A levels and ended up with a degree. I love happy endings.

Lynda revealed that story the next time we met, which was in 2008, at the Chichester rehearsals for the original tour of *Calendar Girls*. That was another memorable day. I also chatted to Brigit Forsyth and Patricia Hodge. Needless to say, the show went on to be a huge hit.

Four years later the *Calendar Girls* was again on tour and coming to the Mayflower, Southampton. I was put in touch with the PR guy and he promised he would set up a few interviews. It never happened. After the press night in Southampton I went backstage to say a quick hello to some of the girls. Out came Lynda, Ruth Madoc, Sue Holderness and Jan Harvey – and I knew all of them.

Lynda immediately said: "John, didn't you want to interview us this time?" When I explained he had never got back to me, after his initial promise, she added: "He's ✱✱✱✱ anyway." She then gave me her email and said she would set it up for me at Woking, in a couple of weeks' time. True to her word, I turned up at Woking and was put in a room with Lynda, Ruth, Sue and Jan. I could have stayed for hours – but they had another show to do.

Over the years Lynda, a truly wonderful lady, received more than her fair share of national publicity and the newspapers always referred to her as 'the Oxo mum.' That annoyed me so much. She was such a talented actor and deserved more recognition than a continual reference to a television commercial. I interviewed her several times and never ever bothered to mention it.

When *At Home With The Braithwaites* was a hit television series I used to sit and admire the brilliant acting of three ladies, in particular. Some of the scenes between Lynda, Amanda Redman and Sylvia Syms were just mesmerising.

I even sometimes tuned in to see her on Loose Woman – but that must remain a secret.

Like millions of others, I was saddened by her death, after such a brave fight.

Thankfully, I have a few memories to cherish.

CHAPTER 39

Freddie Starr

BACK IN 1982 I WONDERED just why all the fuss had been made about Freddie Starr, both on and off stage. The national press had labelled him 'filthy and blue' and looked upon him as a pretty unsociable character. I'd originally been blown away by his talents, like millions of others, on the 1970 Royal Variety Show when he stole the evening from the old guard like Marty Feldman, Leslie Crowther, Max Bygraves and Sandy Powell.

Freddie was not renowned for his love of gentlemen from the press. In his estimation they were far from being gentlemen and he described them quite differently. In '82 I had a real stroke of luck. His manager was my old mate Leon Fisk, once of the sensational Dallas Boys. He ruled his artists with a rod of iron and told Freddie he had to see me. Come the day and it all happened just perfectly and Freddie even thanked me for the interview.

Mr Starr loved an audience and we chatted like old mates because the girl singer from the show was in his dressing room and he wanted to show off a bit. Who could blame him as he was filling theatres all over Britain. It happened again a year or two later and, despite having a touch of 'flu, he insisted on seeing me.

When Leon Fisk gave up being his manager I never got another look in. Not even when Freddie was only eight minutes away in a theatre down the road.

Being from Liverpool he had a great voice and sang in local pop groups for a while and then formed his own Freddie Starr and the Midnighters.

His impressions had begun at school when he took off the teachers and got caned.

I was expecting a punch line and got one: "Now I get paid for it and get caned by the press," said Freddie.

He got fired from the local shipyard and I loved his stories of those struggling times. As an entertainer he earned £15 a week and had a manager he never saw for three years and he wouldn't even pay £6 for a new suit for Freddie to play the Odd Spot, Liverpool.

In London he was later booked for the Victoria Palace and it proved a great break. Even then he was tagged blue and his agent earned his commission by not taking no for an answer.

When he first arrived at the stage door he said in his broad scouse accent: "I'm Freddie Starr," the doorman replied "Fred Astaire?" On being told again he replied:" Who? Never heard of you." Freddie retorted: "Only my mother has."

The band leader took a disliking to young Starr and played his Cliff Richard music in the wrong tempo. Freddie jumped into the pit and broke his baton in two. "It was him or me," he added.

The first time I met Freddie he was making a comeback after five months off. Ten years of valium had taken its toll.

"It takes three years to come off them. I've been without them for 12 months. At one time I was taking 300 milligrams a day. You have to wean off them slowly or you end up at the funny farm. It's a new illness and they don't know what the withdrawal symptoms are."

Sadly, Freddie has suffered unwanted problems in the past few years and his genuine showbiz pals have worried about him. The national press have still hounded him.

So, nothing changes.

CHAPTER 40

Jack Douglas

THE FIRST TIME I ever saw Jack Douglas, away from our television screens, was back in 1981. There were a host of famous stars filming a TV movie called *The End Of The End Of The Pier Show*. Other than Jack, these included Peggy Mount and Norman Vaughan. I saw them in their lunch break at the Cliff Tops Hotel. They had been filming on the nearby Shanklin seafront. On that day, he didn't have Alf Ipititimus with him and there was a not twitch in sight. It was still a right carry on though!

Fifteen years later he came back for a summer season on the Isle of Wight – and, virtually, never went home again. Falling in love with cast member Vivien Russell, a talented all-round entertainer who lived in Shanklin, must have helped him make up his mind. Over the years I got to know him as a close personal friend and he did so much for local charities. He loved attending the local *County Press Theatre Awards* presentation evenings and never missed one until he became unwell. During the latter stage of Jack's eventful life I decided to name one of the annual awards after him. So it became, *The Jack Douglas Award For The Best Comedy*.

One of the saddest days of our friendship was when I went to visit him at the nursing home where he was being cared for. At that stage, he was unable to speak. I told him about naming the comedy award after him and I knew he was proud because he started to cry with emotion. What a pair we were, because I cried for him.

Jack was such a funny guy and he teamed up in a double act with Joe Baker and during a 1955 show at Butlin's, Clacton, Alf Ipititimus was born. Jack, who was already on the stage doing his cod conjuring act, had to improvise very quickly as Joe, who was due to join him from the audience as a little boy, had been accidently locked out of the theatre.

Joe eventually left to try for a solo career in America. Jack then became a straight man for comedians like, Bruce Forsyth, Arthur Haynes and Arthur Askey. Jack eventually left the business to open his own restaurant in Blackpool. Then he was tempted back to stage work by Des O'Connor and they had a double act for 12 years. It was a dream pairing and they ended up on America's *Ed Sullivan Show*, the world's most successful television variety show, and they also stole a *Royal Variety Show*.

Jack was always destined for showbusiness and at the age of 11 he ran away from home to find a job at Feldman's Theatre, Blackpool. He became a lime boy for less than £2 a week.

"My father eventually found out where I was and asked the manager to give me all the dirty jobs, so I would go back home. There weren't any, as far as I was concerned, and I never went back to school," said Jack.

His dad, a theatre director and impresario, gave in to Jack and as a present for his 15th birthday he was allowed to direct a pantomime at the Empire, Sunderland. It proved quite a shock for the cast.

When Jack died in late 2008 it was such a tribute to him that so many stars turned up at the Actor's Church in Covent Garden, the following year, to celebrate his life. These included Barbara Windsor, Wendy Craig, Lynda Baron, Jean Fergusson and Lance Percival. Rick Wakeman read the lesson and Anita Harris did a eulogy.

CHAPTER 41

Larry Grayson

WHILE HOLIDAYMAKING in Torbay in September 1976 I went backstage at a Paignton theatre to look up an old friend who was in a summer show at the resort. I asked him what were the chances of chatting to Larry Grayson, who was starring in a rival show just a mile or two up the road.

He replied: "Not much. I suggest you forget the idea altogether. In any case you won't even get by the chauffeur."

Two days later while going to interview Moira Anderson at the Princess Theatre, I passed Larry Grayson on the stairs. He smiled and said: "Good evening" and was gone. Had I been misled?

It took me six years to find out that I had been. The fact was, Larry Grayson was as nice off stage as he was on.

During the early run of his high-season summer show at Sandown Pavilion I was invited to meet him at a posh hotel in nearby Shanklin. Over morning coffee he proved the perfect host and was more like a favourite uncle than a comedy superstar.

Larry just never stopped talking and had been in love with the theatre since standing on a table and singing along to Layton and Johnstone records. At the age of five he was taken to see *Babes In The Wood* and in his own words: "I thought this was the magic land."

He was adopted as a child and times were hard for the family who brought him up. They couldn't afford music lessons or to send him to a dancing school.

Larry told me: "That didn't stop me. I wanted to be a star one day. All I could do was talk. In the end I talked my way to the Palladium."

For Larry – or Billy Breen as he was once billed – it all began in variety theatres and there he stayed as a virtual unknown until their eventual demise. Then it was tatty clubs, summer concert parties and pubs.

I asked him if it took him 30 years to be discovered? "More like 300," suggested Larry. It took a live *Saturday Variety* television show to introduce 'Everard' and 'Slack Alice' to a mass audience. The rest is well chronicled history.

"I'm glad I wasn't born any later. I was lucky enough to see the best of theatre and films. Nor would I have wanted to miss seeing my name so small on the bill. It would have meant not getting to know some wonderful people."

He continued: "Sadly, when you are a star people don't approach you like they do when you are an ordinary act. I used to go out with everyone in the show. The star always stayed in the hotel like I do now."

A few days earlier he'd been mobbed in the local newspaper shop. The blue rinse brigade took some stopping.

Larry asked me to bring a few friends to his dressing room, after a show, for a nightcap. Among them I took Keith Newbery, my mentor, who had given me such a chance seven years earlier to write a showbiz column. Larry did a 60-minute private cabaret in his snazzy dressing gown. Clutching a glass of Wincarnis and a cigarette holder he was wonderfully unstoppable.

It was also nice for him to met two locals, Grace Adams and Jan Fletcher, who were dancers in a show with him back in the '50s, when he was unknown.

CHAPTER 42

Lionel Bart

LIKE MANY OTHER TEENAGERS of the time, I loved Tommy Steele. He was our first home grown rock 'n' roll star. His dreams were far beyond that burgeoning music scene and he proved it by becoming a world famous star in movies and stage musicals. Tommy's early success was also due to songwriter Lionel Bart, who penned him some great hits. Then Lionel also became world famous as the writer of *Oliver*.

I had the video and the movie soundtrack of *Oliver* and never tired of the brilliant songs. I was in my car one day and some of them came on the radio – and an idea was born. I wondered if Les Reed could come up trumps again? I rang Les and he said the words I wanted to hear: "Just leave it to me." Within a couple of weeks I was in Lionel's flat in Acton.

When I arrived at his door he greeted me warmly, but immediately revealed he had not been well. Thankfully, as I'd come a long way, he was still keen to see me. This was long before mobile phones and emails. He was quite honest and said he might have to nip to the bathroom a few times. Luckily, it didn't happen.

Lionel's story had been well circulated and I'd planned to coax a few different stories out of him and he was up for it. There were so many rumours about his legendary parties.

"It really was swinging London when I had my huge house in Chelsea. The Rolling Stones and the Beatles were always dropping in and Justin Hayward and his girlfriend lived there for a while. Sometimes I was a guest at my own parties and often when I woke up in the morning there were about 15 people around, who'd stayed the night. My parties went on for days. Now I wake up at the time I used to go to bed.

"The Beatles would come and test their songs out on me. Paul played me the tune for *Yesterday* and thought he copied it from somewhere – but he hadn't. I think he called it 'scrambled eggs' at the time, with no real lyric."

The tabloids were always full of Lionel's suspected romantic links with Judy Garland and, in particular Alma Cogan. He told me: "I was very close to Alma. I was also close to Judy but not in the same way."

Just before I visited him he'd been to an event to mark the sad closing of Tin Pan Alley and he was treated as the doyen of Denmark Street, following the huge success of

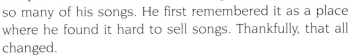

so many of his songs. He first remembered it as a place where he found it hard to sell songs. Thankfully, that all changed.

"I was so very moved when the newer stars like Suggs and Damon Albarn came up to me and told me they'd been influenced, either directly or indirectly, by my songs. Ray Davies said the same thing."

Amazingly, in the early days of his musical *Oliver*, then named *Oliver My Dear*, none of the 12 major theatre managements in London wanted it. A few years later, thanks to the Mermaid Theatre and Sean Kenny and Peter Coe, it became a worldwide hit. The movie won six Oscars.

I love the story of how he saw a doll that walked, talked and peed, advertised in a Sunday paper. He was on a deadline for another song for the Cliff Richard movie *Serious Charge* and he wrote *Living Doll* in just 15 minutes.

Just before I went, I played him the Barron Knights parody of *Little White Bull*, called *Little White Bum*. He'd never heard that before and loved it.

CHAPTER 43

Michael Parkinson

SOME SAY YOU SHOULD NEVER meet your idols. In my case that was put to the test on Sunday September 17, 1978. Michael Parkinson was booked for a Sunday Concert at Sandown Pavilion. I was such a fan of his television chat show and loved his relaxed style of gently prodding his guests into conversation topics that made his show so unique. How that technique has changed in more recent years, when the hosts now look on themselves as the stars and often just use their guests as fodder for cheap laughs. Hence, my off switch is instantly applied when the likes of Jonathan Ross come on my television screen.

Would 'Parky' be arrogant and full of his own importance? Would he even bother with a small time showbiz writer for a local paper, who also did voluntary hospital radio? The friendliness of his welcome and his interest in my fledgling career relaxed me instantly. I'd only been interviewing for around two years. Nothing was too much trouble. He gave me two interviews in one. He talked about his career as a chat show host and also of his great love for sport. I also had a Sports Personality column in the *Isle of Wight Weekly Post* and he was the first to appear in both.

In those days you could often chance your arm and just turn up with a cassette recorder. His agent Dabber Davis was with him and readily agreed that Michael would do the interview. During our chat I brought up the subject of his renowned interviewing technique. I then had a goosebumps moment. The great Parkinson told me I was a good interviewer because I looked at people when I asked questions, listened to their reply and did my research. I have never forgotten that advice over 4,000 interviews later.

I loved the stories he told me. When he was working on a Yorkshire weekly paper, as a naive young reporter, he was asked to cover a society wedding and could barely wait to see his story in print – and he had his first byline. His joy was somewhat subdued when he noticed an embarrassing error. He had written: "The bridegroom gave his bride an electric clock." The last word, as printed, was minus the l – and a note went around the office that in future clocks would be referred to as time pieces. True or not, it was a great story.

Years later I was thrilled to meet George Best, who owed such a lot to Michael, and during our interview he went out of his way to pay tribute to a guy he looked on as a real mentor. After our interview, George and Rodney Marsh dashed back to the mainland to make guest appearances at a charity cricket match and Michael was involved in that game.

He also told me of the time in a Yorkshire League cricket match when a weedy, frail kid, who was even wearing glasses, came out to the wicket and his arrival produced a few moments of humour from the fielding team. The youngster had the last laugh – and they couldn't get him out. His name was Geoffrey Boycott.

I asked 'Parky' for an embarrassing moment. Apparently, he'd always wanted to seduce Shirley MacLaine. She was booked for his TV show and he thought he was doing quite well. I'll let him finish the story.

"Suddenly Shirley brought me down. She stuck her finger into my belly button and said: 'You have a shirt button missing.' I have never blushed so much." Needless to say, his dream remained just that.

CHAPTER 44

Mike and Bernie Winters

MORECAMBE AND WISE were by far Britain's most popular television comedy double act, when millions watched every show. As live stage performers, Mike and Bernie Winters ran them very close and in some people's estimation were actually the funnier act in front of a live audience. They certainly wowed thousands at Sandown Pavilion in their 1978 summer season. It was a gamble that show producer John Redgrave bravely took and it was well justified, as the sold out boards regularly proved. I had never seen so many people in one place crying with laughter.

Mike and Bernie seen here at their last ever appearance together.

What many punters did not realise that summer was that the two brothers were not speaking anymore off stage. It was hard to contemplate how two brothers could not talk to each other before or after a show and yet for 50 minutes on stage they never stopped talking to one another.

I'd done the usual pre-opening plug in my showbiz column in the *Isle of Wight Weekly Post* and the first night review, but decided to hold the major interview until their final week. It appeared the day before their last ever stage appearance together, which was on Saturday September 16, 1978.

I sensed problems were ahead when I discovered they had separate dressing rooms and did not relish being interviewed together. One would not speak for the other. In the end, there was a compromise and they even had a picture taken together – and they were both smiling.

Their last show together was an amazing night and they were so funny and the 1000-strong audience loved every minute.

Bernie had told me a few days earlier: "We could never wish to close at a better place. These Sandown audiences have been the most consistently good in all our 30 years together. You would think we were just starting not disbanding. We are going out with flying colours."

On that final Saturday night the boys sang "wherever we go, we go together" on the Sandown Pavilion stage – but within a few minutes they had parted. That final show must have been the most emotional in all their 30 years together. They had camouflaged any bottled-up emotion until the final rapturous applause suddenly unleashed the real sadness of the occasion.

Both quickly moved on to new solo careers. Virtually just after their Sandown finale Mike jetted off to America where he was due to host two pilot quiz shows and write for television. A chat show was another possibility.

Bernie, who came back on several occasions to top the bill as a solo comedian, had completely changed his attitude and was a real pleasure to talk to. I loved his company. On one visit he was actually pictured on the front of the current TV *Times* for his new television series. It could be that old wounds had still not healed.

He told me." I hope my brother sees that in America because he won't like that very much."

I was then photographed with his new partner – Snorbitz. They hit it off a lot better. Bernie, however, did reveal the secret that there was more than just one Snorbitz.

CHAPTER 45

Fenella Fielding

IN 2011, I WAS SENT a press release with regard to a new book called *Carry On Actors*, which had been written by Andrew Ross. There were interview slots available with the author. With due respect to Mr Ross, I got more excited when I noticed the foreword was written by Fenella Fielding. For us guys of a certain age, her stunning looks and sexy voice would never be forgotten.

I contacted Fenella's agent and he was so helpful. He quickly got back to me with the exciting news that she would be happy to be interviewed near her home in Chiswick. At this stage, I had mentioned it would be a recorded interview for a radio show. The arrangements were made and I was told Fenella would love to do it in a nice little French-style cafe near her home, which she was familiar with.

The day arrived, which just happened to be her birthday, so I made a point of buying some flowers en route. I arrived early and walked to the chosen venue from Turnham Green underground station. I was a little concerned when I discovered it was really a cake and bread shop, with a few tables. The door bell that rang every couple of minutes was not really ideal for an intimate interview with a movie star.

Fenella arrived looking rather glamorous and far younger than her actual age. We found a table and she said: "John, this is for a magazine isn't it?" Somehow communication wires had been crossed and she was unaware it was for a radio chat show. She clearly looked distressed and suggested we went outside to take a breather to try and sort out our problem.

"Obviously, we need somewhere quiet and this might prove difficult. There is a church nearby so perhaps we could go in there. If not, there is a hotel down the road and they might be able to help us," said a flustered Fenella.

As we crossed the busy road I noticed a theatre pub quite nearby, which was called The Tabard, and wondered if they might be able to help. By sheer luck a guy came out of the theatre and I rushed over to catch him. I explained I had come up from the Isle of Wight to do an interview and that the nearby cake shop was not the ideal location. He then looked across the car park and excitedly said: "That's Fenella Fielding over there!" When I told him I'd come up to interview her, he quickly disappeared and came back a few minutes later to tell us we could use their office and that he'd turned the phones off so we wouldn't get disturbed.

So, thanks to The Tabard, a very successful Turnham Green theatre pub, we were given coffee and the use of their office for the duration of the interview. I'm no fool – and we didn't come out for at least 50 minutes.

We had fun and there was so much to talk about, including her hit movies with Tony Curtis and Dirk Bogarde, being labelled Britain's first lady of double entendre, the Carry On films, Morecambe and Wise and some amazing straight theatre roles.

Since first making *Carry On Screaming* she'd never been far away from one particular line: "Do you mind if I smoke?" Even youngsters who were not even born at the time, come up to her and quote the words she spoke to Harry H Corbett.

Fenella was also the first actress to be used by Morecambe and Wise on their TV shows. Once again, she had a classic line when she made a play for Little Ern, much to the delight of Eric. "Darling, I love them when they're small. They're half the work and twice the fun."

CHAPTER 46

Frank Carson

HAVE YOU HEARD THE ONE about the Irishman who kept leaping out of an aircraft over Albany Barracks on the Isle of Wight in late 1944. It was 36 years before he returned to his wartime location. This time without his parachute and in his new role as one of Britain's most-loved comedians. He was a 'cracker' alright – and his name was Frank Carson.

The first time I met Frank was in early 1980 and I never stopped laughing throughout his act or the interview. He loved meeting people on and off stage. Some comedians have been known as miserable recluses away from the job but Frank was just the opposite. He told me: "If anybody walks by me in the street and doesn't recognise me, I run after them, stop them and do a 20-minute spot."

I last met Frank in 2012 and on that occasion he asked me if I would pick him up from the ferry and take him to the plush Warner's Bembridge Coast Hotel. I didn't say much in the 20-minute drive to the venue – only when he took a quick breath. He had even more to say at the hotel when he was told there was not a room for him. It was a genuine error but he was not happy. To compensate, as he was their star cabaret, they offered him a room at the nearby Crab and Lobster. I talked him out of heading straight back to the ferry and took him to the pub. He loved the room and we did an instant interview. Then we went down into the bar and, of course, he did a quick 20 minutes before I drove him back to Bembridge Coast Hotel.

The cabaret room was full to capacity and Frank brought the house down. They loved his spot of at least an hour or more. I then drove him back to the pub and when I finally left for home he was still doing an impromptu comedy session in their bar.

During our interview at the pub he'd again referred to his wartime stint on the Isle of Wight but this time he had a confession to make via my radio show. It concerned a lady called Emily. I wondered just what was coming next but, luckily, it was being pre-recorded and I would be able to edit, if necessary.

"The night before I left the Isle of Wight for Palestine in late 1944 I told this beautiful young lady called Emily that I would be back to see her and would she wait for me. She told me she would but that was 68 years ago. I wonder if she's still waiting." The radio station never had a phone call – so she must have given up. I just wondered if she ever realised when she saw Frank on television that he was her one-time wartime fella from Albany Barracks.

Spike Milligan once said: "If Frank's vocal chords were in his legs, he'd be in a wheelchair."

In England Frank first found real fame on *The Comedians*, but he had already been a hit in Ireland and appeared in hundreds of television shows. Such was his fame, following *The Comedians*, he even went to the States to appear on the *Johnny Carson Show*.

During his years of stardom, many leading politicians and celebrities would have received a Carson letter or telegram. He loved writing to them. Fans who wrote to Frank were so surprised to get a handwritten reply. He would put his private address at the top so they could keep in touch.

Frank, so renowned for his charity work, did much to enhance people's lives. When he met The Pope it must have been a surprise for both of them.

CHAPTER 47

Bill Maynard

I'D ALWAYS BEEN A FAN of Bill Maynard since I first saw him in *Great Scott It's Maynard*, a popular television series from the mid '50s, when he was famous for his big sweaters, as well as his great flair for comedy. Then much later came Greengrass in *Heartbeat*. I had briefly met him on the day England won the World Cup in 1966. He was appearing in a Bournemouth summer season production of *Lock Up Your Daughters* at the Palace Court Theatre with Craig Douglas and Ann Sidney. I went to see the evening performance and was invited backstage, by Craig, to meet the cast.

I interviewed Bill for the first time at the Kings Theatre, Southsea, in 1987, when he was playing Daddy Warbucks in *Annie*. He proved an interviewer's dream before the matinee and just never stopped talking. My wife had gone on into the show with her ticket and I suddenly realised during our chat that the show had started and was some way in. I had overlooked the fact that Bill did not go on very early in the musical and had time to kill.

Bill was so fascinating to talk to. He'd been prepared to take risks and they paid off. Despite being a huge light entertainment star, he decided in the '50s, as the variety theatres were on the wane, to give up his £1,000 a week salary, at the time we spoke that equated to around £17,000 a week, to earn just £50 a week in repertory. Not surprisingly, it eventually meant he went broke and became known as a has-been.

There had been heated arguments with his management but Bill got his way and that £950 a week drop in salary! His acting career started in sleepy Worthing. The play was *You Too Can Have A Body* and by the Wednesday it was earmarked for the West End. It was not Bill's idea of a dream part. He had designs on playing Davis in Pinter's *The Caretaker*, but he took the chance. His tours in rep eventually led to him bankruptcy. Then came a tax demand from his years of stardom.

"I was going round the country getting artistic accolades but no money. Sometimes I doubled with working men's clubs. Playing them was fine, when you were going up, but on the way down they look on you as a has-been. That's what the public thought as well. It was very hard."

There had been some resentment at times with the theatricals. One company walked out because they wouldn't work with a variety person.

Out of the blue, he was offered the role of a journalist in Dennis Potter's TV play *Paper Roses*. Following that came Colin Welland's BAFTA-winning *Kisses At Fifty* and then his huge hits *The Life Of Riley*, *Oh No, It's Selwyn Froggitt*, *The Gaffer* and *Heartbeat*.

"I became a one-off. I was the only character actor who became a name. Those who are, basically big names, play the same part for ever.

"You have to go out and make it happen."

The last time I met Bill was in a 1996 Guildford pantomime. He was lying on a sofa in his dressing room and I lowered his microphone so he didn't have to move. The assistant stage manager came in and he asked her to go shopping but she told him it was too near show time. I volunteered and he gave me a £10 note to get a toothbrush, toothpaste and soap. I got back and gave him the change. "Blimey, I'll send you again. They never bring me back any change."

CHAPTER 48

Su Pollard

THE FIRST TIME I MET SU POLLARD, I said nothing at all, although I had anticipated her bursting in on an interview. The setting was a pantomime at the Mayflower, Southampton and I was recording an interview with Michael Elphick, so famous for that brilliant *Boon* series. He had pre-warned me that Miss Pollard had arrived in the building and might be doing the rounds. Suddenly the door opened and in she came. She saw the red microphone, apologised profusely and made a hasty exit. We didn't worry at all. How could you get cross with such an adorable lady as Su Pollard?

I did eventually catch up with Su in Brighton, Worthing and Aylesbury. I never said much in any of those interviews. She's nothing like Meg Ryan, who gave Parky such a hard time. It was a woman called Peggy Ollerenshaw in that classic holiday camp series H*i-de-H*i that changed her life forever. Su and Ruth Madoc, who played Gladys Pugh,

became such iconic television characters. The whole series was brimful of such gifted actors. My favourite episode is T*he Day Of Reckoning*, when a panto horse rides a real horse, with the classic banana and whisky scene featuring Mr Partridge, superbly played by Leslie Dwyer.

Su will always be grateful for those eight years in H*i-de*-Hi. She told me: "We all embraced what was offered us. It was such a great show to be a part of and it was so exciting to be giving millions of people so much pleasure."

The very next morning after the first-ever transmission she was completely taken by surprise in her local London market. People stared at her and she was asked for autographs. They were also surprised when she talked to them in a very posh voice – and she still doesn't know why she did that.

"One day I was up a mountain in Greece and a local man came up to me and said 'hi-de-hi.' I said how do you know about that and he told me his brother had a chip shop in Birmingham and he'd seen me on his television."

Whenever I meet Su at a theatre, I'm never quite sure whether she's dressed for the show or just come in from the street. I love her outfits and she always rattles her beads for my radio listeners. She has a huge gay following and they love touching her beads.

When people see Su in a show like S*hout* they are stunned by the quality and power of her voice. She actually had a Top Three record with S*tarting Together*. In the early days of Isle of Wight Radio we had a young guy called Stu McGinley who loved Su's hit record but we weren't allowed to mention it. Street cred and all that. I did let it slip, deliberately.

Amazingly, when Su was 16, she appeared as a solo act in Northern clubs and they loved her. She could really belt out a song and wore hot pants on stage. A few years later she won a national rear of the year title.

"I got a tray for that with a picture of my bum on it. I always bring it out at Christmas to serve the drinks on," quipped Su. I presume she meant the tray!!

Her career has been so diverse. In the '70s she toured with matinee singing idol John Hanson and has played Miss Hannigan in A*nnie*. Whilst playing this role she flew out to Benidorm on a Sunday, filmed a guest spot in the hit TV series on the Monday and jetted back to A*nnie* for the Tuesday night show. Su also presented S*ongs Of Praise* on a couple of occasions.

CHAPTER 49

Syd Lawrence

INSTEAD OF BLOWING MY OWN TRUMPET to celebrate interviewing Syd Lawrence, after more than four years of trying, I blew his instead. Syd took it all in his stride and even jotted down a few notes, mainly flat ones, to take a leaf out of my book.

My early February 1980 'speak to me Syd Lawrence press campaign' and the kindness of the local West Wight Rotary Club helped to finally realise an assignment that was beginning to haunt me. I had tried so many times and could not even get past his manager. I think my determination finally won the day. In hindsight, the long wait was worth it. I enjoyed his company immensely and he gave me more time than Joe Loss had done in 1976.

My late father, Roy, was also delighted. He was a great lover of the big band era and, long before I was born, he and mum would cycle miles to see the famous big bands in action. They would come home from late night gigs and barely see a car on the road.

When I finally met Syd, he emphasised how the past 11 years had been beyond his wildest dreams. From being somewhat bored, playing big band pop in the BBC's Northern Dance Orchestra, he suddenly found world fame with his re-creation of the Glenn Miller sound.

"At the end of the '60s the big bands, as I knew them, had disappeared and pop had taken over. I wasn't particularly happy playing that type of music. It just didn't fit in with anything I wanted to do."

Syd Lawrence with John on the trumpet

Unable to perform his favourite music for a living, Syd decided to play it purely for kicks, one night a week, in his leisure time. So his first 'fun band' was formed. News of this talented unit spread like a plague and they were soon in great demand. Once on television they never looked back.

"I was in a bit of a quandary. Did I leave the NDO after 16 years and take a chance, at my time of life, with my own band?"

It proved an inspired decision and Syd was back on the road again. His earliest musical training had been on a cornet in a pre-war brass band. During the war he'd served in the RAF, the uniformed hot-bed of talented musicians. He ended up playing in the big band in Cairo alongside many pro musicians,

He reflected: "I had to suddenly pull my finger out and do my best. It was okay and I got the scene. Also I learnt to arrange music for big bands."

Later during his NDO days he helped back great stars like Eddie Fisher, Debbie Reynolds and Billy Eckstine.

The amazing success of the Syd Lawrence Orchestra even took him by surprise and all their gigs were sell-outs.

"There is only room for one or two bands on a revival kick. We were just lucky to get in first. Nothing was planned. It's so sad that many others have tried it since and failed."

I wondered whether his latest album, at that time, *McCartney – His Music – And Me*, was a deliberate policy to update the band's music. In other words, to stop them being typecast. My assumption was somewhat off-key. In fact Syd never wanted to record an album of McCartney's songs. It was inflicted on him by Philips Records.

That led directly to Syd, in partnership with his recording manager, to form their own label. He added:"I now listen to my fans and my albums are called *At Your Request.*"

CHAPTER 50

Sylvia Syms

BACK IN THE MID '70s, when I still had a day job as a salesman for United Biscuits, I was sent on a two-day seminar to Bristol. Being teetotal, I was not interested in visiting any local nightclubs or just staying in the hotel drinking pints. I drove to the Theatre Royal, Bath, in time to catch Sylvia Syms coming out of the stage door, where she was appearing in a touring play. At the time I had a programme on our local hospital radio network. She came out and with no hesitation, after being asked for an interview, took me inside to record around 10 minutes on my cassette recorder. I was missed from the hotel and had to confess where I'd been. The following morning I was asked to play the interview to the other guys and they all clapped at the end, which embarrassed me.

It was fully 40 years later before I met her again. I went to her London home and once again she made me very welcome and we barely stopped laughing for a couple of hours. I loved her frankness and she spoke openly about so many things. I had a quick tour before we started and her memorabilia was so fascinating. To prove Sylvia could make anyone laugh, there was a picture of her with the Queen and Her Majesty had a huge smile on her face.

"I love the Queen. To me she epitomises duty and honesty and I find her incredible. I didn't tell her I played the Queen Mum in the Helen Mirren movie."

Sylvia was always prepared to learn from more experienced actors during her early days in the business and she remembered Dame Edith Evans, Anna Neagle and Laurence Harvey with particular pleasure.

In over 60 years Sylvia had made at least 50 movies. At the time of my visit she had just celebrated her 81st birthday. I loved *Ice Cold In Alex*. Once again, the stars were so kind to her. John Mills, Anthony Quayle and Harry Andrews really looked after her. They certainly complained bitterly when they discovered that when the ambulance ran downhill towards her it was not on a hawser, as they were promised. It was just as well she rolled away right on cue.

At the time of the film's release there was much publicity about some love scenes, between Sylvia and John Mills, that had been removed.

"It was all a myth really. There was nothing to it. I may have had one more button undone but that was all. Nowadays they can do anything."

The Tamarind Seed was also a big movie for her. It starred Omar Sharif and Julie Andrews and that rekindled more memories for Sylvia.

"You can get prejudiced ideas about people and I thought Julie Andrews might be a kind of stuffed shirt. Actually, she was so funny and sharp and had a mouth like a trucker. I thought she was sensational."

She also told me Dirk Bogarde was the crème de la crème and she loved working with him in *Victim*, a movie he was very brave to appear in.

Sylvia made a movie for Michael Winner called A *Chorus Of Disapproval*. That question brought a quick response: "Shall we pass on now. He had a marvellous cast, too. He didn't do well on that one and it was about as funny as a cup of cold sick."

I also asked her about a mutual friend, the late cinematographer Gil Taylor, who worked on *Ice Cold In Alex*. She thought he was brilliant – and I couldn't agree more.

I didn't want to leave her house. It was fun from start to finish. I'd love to go back and meet her very talented daughter, Beatie Edney.

CHAPTER 51

Bruce Forsyth

TOP TELEVISION SCRIPTWRITER Wally Malston had a dream for me to interview his good friend Bruce Forsyth. Wally was involved with several of his hit television shows like *You Bet!*, *Play Your Cards Right* and *The Generation Game*. The Palladium legend offered me a telephone interview but I wanted the thrill of meeting him. So things had gone quiet.

Sadly, Wally became seriously ill and was in the Phyllis Tuckwell Memorial Hospice in Farnham. Bruce thought so much of him and visited Wally within hours of returning from his winter break in Puerto Rico.

Wally passed away and we went to the funeral at the Aldershot Crematorium. It was my first showbiz funeral and lots of stars were there. Bruce did an amazing eulogy, full of fun, which Wally would have loved. Their friendship had been much more than just a star and his scriptwriter.

Ted Rogers introduced me to Bruce outside of the crematorium and when he heard my name he said: "I know you were a great friend of Wally's and didn't we do an interview?" I had to say that it had not taken place. Then I found myself saying wouldn't it be nice to do one and dedicate it to Wally's memory.

Bruce loved the idea to celebrate Wally's life with the radio interview and gave me his home phone number with instructions to call him in about six week's time as he was going to the West Indies. I duly called him after those few weeks and he was a little unsure when he could do it, but we sort of made a provisional date. I got home from work one evening and Sean was so excited. Bruce had rung up and asked: "Is your dad in, son? This is Bruce Forsyth."

I had to ring Bruce back but he was rather cagey and said it might be alright for the following Monday, our suggested day, but hinted he would have to confirm it, as something was about to crop up. A couple of days later he did ring to confirm I could still come up to his home, as planned. In those few days, in-between, he'd been awarded the MBE and was a little uncertain of his movements. He obviously knew, but couldn't tell me until it was official.

En route to his delightful house, my mobile phone rang. I pulled into a lay-by to take the call, which was from Felix Bowness. He had also been to Wally's funeral and was so thrilled for me that Bruce had kept his promise. I think he rang to see if I could get him some work! Well he cheered me up, as I was a little nervous, and put me in the perfect mood to interview a genuine British superstar.

Bruce was a little delayed but had arranged for coffee and biscuits while I waited. I set up my equipment, with two microphone stands, and mine was positioned over a table full of ornaments and personal treasures. It wasn't until on the way home that I suddenly thought what would have happened if it had collapsed.

Bruce was all I could have imagined. A perfect host and willing to give me over an hour of his valuable time. We really hit it off and I'm sure Wally would have known we had finally got together. He willingly talked about his early days, his struggles to find any sort of fame and then, of course, his arrival as the compère of *Sunday Night At The London Palladium*. He did ask if I could leave out one or two of my planned records, particularly some of his own 'poppy' things, which he didn't like. It all worked out perfectly and he even asked for a CD copy of the programme.

CHAPTER 52

Bernie Clifton

I FIRST MET BERNIE CLIFTON back in the summer of 1983, at a Sunday Concert at Sandown Pavilion. He willingly gave me an interview despite a remarkable journey just to even get there. On the Saturday night he walked off stage on Blackpool's South Pier and within 15 minutes began heading for the Isle of Wight. Those lucky enough to have seen his two performances on Sandown Pier the following day were not aware of his manic weekend.

He drove the 200 miles to Swindon from the Rockin' Berries Blackpool Show and arrived around 2am. On the road again at 10am he drove the 100 miles to Portsmouth, caught the car ferry to Fishbourne for a 4pm band call. Over a quick chicken salad we chatted for a few minutes before the first show.

On the road again, after his two shows, he caught the 11.45pm ferry to Portsmouth and then drove the 250 miles non-stop to his Chesterfield home. Following a few hours sleep he was back on the road and driving 150 miles to Blackpool for two Monday night shows. Showbiz stars have an easy life? Don't you believe it!

Bernie was very shrewd. He must have felt like a rally driver covering 700 miles for two 20-minute spots. They proved a perfect showcase and earned him a very successful 1984 summer season on the Isle of Wight and numerous one-nighters over the following years.

I quickly discovered Bernie Clifton was mad on and off stage. During our salad snack he completely lost control of the chicken portion and forked it up from the floor. A few years later he came live into my radio show and just about made it. They were resurfacing the nearby major roundabout and he'd got lost. He re-lived the saga on air more than once and the listeners loved it.

I've always felt Bernie fell out of a time warp, about 20 years too late. He has the stamp of a real music hall and variety entertainer. Even as a teenager he was making people laugh – and there was not even an ostrich in sight. At his local cinema he used to borrow the doorman's bike and ride it across the cinema stage during the main movie.

Bernie had begun as a band and club singer and, amazingly, he was nervous in those days. He told me: "I used to shut my eyes and grab the microphone stand."

It took him a few years to graduate from being funny off stage to on stage. Some old junkshop props helped him to acclimatise. Many years later his comedy routine saved an ailing 1979 Royal Variety Show.

I saw Bernie perform on so many occasions when summer shows were still in full swing. His ostrich routine was a showstopper but I think he even topped that with his Red Shadow and John Hanson skit, which ended up with a water-filled monkey and a cylinder of gas. Priceless.

Back in 1995 Heather and I drove to Weymouth to see a brilliant summer show which starred Bernie, Ted Rogers and Bonnie Langford. What a show that was and I interviewed all three before curtain up. Then it was my turn to drive fast to get the last ferry back to the Isle of Wight.

CHAPTER 53

Cannon and Ball

IN THE AUTUMN OF 1978, Gene Pitney played Sandown Pavilion and the tickets were sold out in less than three hours. No computers in those days. It was an early morning queue along the seafront. Sadly, Gene was not doing any interviews on the day of the concert. If only I'd known who the supporting cast were. An unknown comedy double act called Cannon and Ball absolutely stormed the audience. They were obviously destined for huge success and it duly came two years later.

I did try and arrange an interview with the boys who, by that time, were the hottest property on Britain's light entertainment scene but could get nowhere near them. They were renowned for not giving many. That all changed in 1986, when they came back to Sandown as megastars. There was a slight problem. Off stage, they were not quite in harmony and I interviewed Tommy Cannon in his dressing room and was told that Bobby Ball might join us. I struck lucky. The guy with the red braces walked in to complete the most successful comedy act since Morecambe and Wise.

They were thrilled to be back at Sandown where they had appeared with Gene Pitney eight years earlier. "That Sandown audience was one of the best we had ever had," enthused Bobby.

Their amazing success story of how they met as welders in a Lancashire factory and became a singing duo, the Harper Brothers, before their emergence as comedy giants Cannon and Ball created stories in many newspapers.

"I think sometimes you get a bit desperate, particularly when you are singers. That's all we did in the early days. We had a few anxious moments when we got paid off or didn't last at the gig. We had each other to lean on," said Tommy.

An accident led them to comedy and their subsequent name change. It was still not easy and they flopped on *Opportunity Knocks*. Their first television series was wiped out by a seven-week strike. They did win *Club Comedy Act Of The Year* three times in a row. The rest is history.

The next time I met them was at Warner's Holiday Centre, Norton Grange, in 2000. They had travelled over by car ferry and were spotted on board by a member of the Isle of Wight Radio news team. He was always looking for a story and followed them in his car to the venue and they were impressed and gave him a short interview. He was then surprised when I turned up for my pre-arranged interview with the duo.

It was such pleasure to meet them again and find they were now closer together than ever before. There had always been rumours about Cannon and Ball and they decided to come clean in their fascinating book. They never spoke for at least four years and stayed in different hotels. The atmosphere at this interview was so different to the previous one back in '86.

Bobby explained: "We regret it now. It was a stupid thing to do. We had a good living in the clubs but when our TV career took off we both let our egos take over and get in the way. We also had people around us chipping away and that didn't help. I don't know why we stayed together."

Tommy made another point: "Strangely, the minute we walked on stage it was fine for the hour and then we went back to living separate lives."

Bobby actually discovered God, which changed his life completely, and Tommy followed seven years later. I had a job to stop them talking and their rapport was so enjoyable. Another happy ending – and they recorded a fantastic personal jingle for my show.

CHAPTER 54

Dennis Waterman

IN THE SUMMER OF 1977, I was a regular at Shanklin Theatre for their Barry O'Brien plays, *Suddenly At Home* and *The Mating Game*, which starred Peter Cleall and a great supporting cast. During the interval of every show they played a new album by Dennis Waterman, called *Down Wind Of Angels*. He was due at one of the Sunday shows. I just loved his rock album and the amazing guest stars who played on it.

Dennis came in peak season and surprised many of his fans who only really knew him as George Carter from the hit series *The Sweeney*. I loved the cult TV show and interrogated Dennis in the theatre's basement. It was the quietest place, as his band were doing a soundcheck on stage.

His new rock album was a far cry from his initial baptism into the music business. That had been in *The Music Man* and there were no twanging guitars in *Seventy Six Trombones* or *'Til There Was You* – and he was only 12 at the time. Three years later he was performing in London clubs and restaurants.

When we met he was keen to make a point about the album: "I would hate people to think I'm another singing policeman actor. I have always been into music. It's not because I'm in a successful TV series and trying to cream a few bob off the top."

At that time he was doing one-night stands, hence his appearance at Shanklin. DJM Records had plans for his recording career and his follow-up album, *Waterman*, was another gem.

Dennis was a gifted rock singer but his television successes that followed *The Sweeney*, like *Minder* and *New Tricks*, meant he was always busy and could not devote much time to his hopes of becoming accepted as a genuine rock star. He did a brilliant job on the memorable theme tunes for both *Minder* and *New Tricks*. The former was written by Gerard Kenny and on one occasion Dennis joined him on stage to sing the song, which can be heard on a Kenny album.

When we met he was filming the last series of *The Sweeney*.

"People have told them they are stupid to finish the programme but the thought of being typecast is always there. We don't want to stay on and become a boring institution.

"The whole unit is such a happy affair and we all go out eating and drinking together and generally take the mick. There is no starry treatment for anyone."

Well over 20 years later Dennis was due to come back to the Isle of Wight for a well-advertised special celebrity appearance at a local hotel. The media arrived and waited for several hours, as we were told he was on his way. It never happened.

Some time after the Shanklin interview I found out that Dennis had been to the Isle of Wight before and nearly drowned. It was told to me by the late Jack Whitehead, the brilliant wood carver and television special effects man.

They were making a movie for the Children's Film Foundation in Shalfleet Creek and young 11 year-old-Dennis was in it. He had to jump into the creek in front of a boat but couldn't swim. During the shooting he failed to jump three times and when he finally made it, he disappeared from view. Suddenly up popped Dennis near the stern of the boat in his yellow lifejacket. The panic was over and a very startled young teenager was safely aboard. Apparently, he did learn to swim after that lucky escape.

CHAPTER 55

Derren Nesbitt

BACK IN 2003, we headed to Eastbourne for a few days, primarily to interview crime writer John Pearson and my long term friend, Wilf Pine, the subject of John's latest book, *One Of The Family*. I had noticed that TV and movie star Derren Nesbitt was in a play at the local Devonshire Park Theatre. Could it happen? I did some research just in case. On the day we arrived we had lunch in Favoloso's, right near the two principal theatres and, by pure chance, Derren Nesbitt was sat in there. I briefly introduced myself and two days later was interviewing him backstage at the theatre.

When we chatted at the Devonshire Park, I asked him if he thought I was a crank when I accosted him in the cafe. "No, I just thought you were after money," quipped Derren.

His father, Harry Nesbitt, was a famous music hall and variety comedian and he worked with his older brother Max as a double act. Derren told me: "I only saw my father on Sundays, as he was always touring theatres around Britain. In the school holidays, he often took me with him and I saw so many great acts."

After RADA, Derren went to the Old Vic at the same time as the young Richard Burton. I just had to ask him what the legendary actor was like in those early days.

"Richard was drunk most of the time. Years later when we were working on *Where Eagles Dare* he was drinking four to five bottles of vodka a day. Once at the Old Vic he told me he was fed up with doing Shakespeare in the theatre and was going to make real money. His interest was primarily in the money. That's what drove him on far more than the acting."

One day at the Old Vic, Richard's car had broken down and Derren offered to drive him home. Burton was surprised he even had a car. Shrewdly, he always parked it out of the way of the theatre.

"He was shocked when he discovered it was my father's Rolls Royce. Richard admitted he could never afford a car like that." That was not the case a few years on.

Derren played the German Von Hapen in *Where Eagles Dare*, alongside giants like Burton and Clint Eastwood. After Derren's cable car scene they deliberately left him up there and he became a bit worried as it started to sway about.

"Incidentally, I actually told the director there were no helicopters in 1941 and he told me they would never know that in Arkansas."

Derren also played a German in *The Naked Runner*, with Frank Sinatra. He had very happy memories of working with the megastar. A tabloid newspaper wanted to pay Derren a lot of money to reveal any stories about Sinatra but he declined the offer. The

legendary crooner found this out and became very friendly with Derren.

"We were going to film one of my scenes in Copenhagen but in the end it was actually Welwyn Garden City. Frank had told me I would love Copenhagen and was disappointed for me. So much so, that he told me he would pay for me to go there for 10 days holiday and I flew out in his private jet. A guy in a grey suit met me at the airport and put a brown paper envelope in my hand. It was spending money and more than enough for 10 days. Every morning he came back to the fantastic hotel and gave me another brown envelope full of money. Frank was so generous."

Later when Sinatra was appearing at the Royal Festival Hall he invited Derren to be on his table at a posh Claridge's pre-show event.

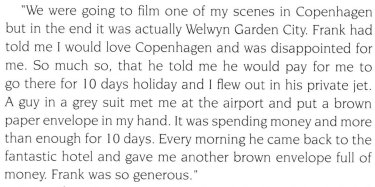

CHAPTER 56

Donald Pleasence

ONE JULY SUNDAY MORNING in the summer of 1980, I met a Russian spy in a secluded Isle of Wight country house, just a mile or so from St Catherine's Lighthouse. This unexpected coup for a mere showbiz columnist was even more sensational because he wasn't going to be exposed until the autumn. Could I keep quiet – or should I ring *The Sun*?

If his face had not been so familiar it would have been much easier to have remained tight-lipped. Where had I seen him before? It was so uncanny. My mind kept going back to movies like *Soldier Blue*, *The Great Escape* and *You Only Live Twice*.

Before you think I'm going quite mad I must reveal that the spy who came in from that warm morning air just happened to be one of my favourite actors, Donald Pleasence. He was playing a spy in the Dennis Potter thriller *Blade On The Feather*.

A couple of nights earlier he had scared the living daylights out of me in a late-night horror movie. All of a sudden there he was in a dingy old room still wearing his dressing gown. Thankfully, he didn't have Blofeld's white cat sat on his lap. We spent about 20 minutes together before he nipped off to check his next lines.

Ironically, exactly 41 years after he'd begun his professional acting career in Jersey, he was back on another small island. So much had happened to Donald during those in-between years. There had been hit West End seasons and top television dramas but movies were his real forte. He'd made over 100 but had forgotten many of them – and some he'd wanted to forget, anyway.

"I actually loved making westerns. The wranglers and Hollywood cowboys are so friendly to work with. You even go and get your coffee on horseback. No-one walks anywhere, "said Donald, whose westerns include *Soldier Blue*, *The Hallelujah Trail* and *Will Penny*. One night I was sat at home watching the latter movie, which also starred Charlton Heston, and I felt so lucky to have interviewed both of them, in-person. They were having an on-screen punch up at the time.

Donald also explained how Hollywood movies were shot so much quicker than in the old days. He spent six months on the filming of *The Greatest Story Ever Told* but his scenes only took 20 days but he stayed around all the time.

One of my own favourite movies is *The Great Escape* and I just had to ask Donald about this classic prisoner of war story. He actually played the forger who was going blind. In his case it was a case of reliving his past. He was imprisoned in a fliers camp in Germany.

"The Great Escape was a good movie but I think we all looked too healthy," suggested Donald.

He also revealed a few surprises which were a million miles from many of his most sinister roles. Among these was the news that he'd written a children's book called *Scouse The Mouse*, which was destined to be a big hit in the States. There was also an album made from it featuring Adam Faith, Barbara Dickson and Ringo Starr.

Before I left I saw a few scenes all ready to roll and Donald being prepared for action. It was not easy filming this spy thriller which had certain similarities to the Anthony Blunt real life story. The clifftop house was under the flight path of jets which kept flying past at the most inconvenient times.

CHAPTER 57

Jeremy Irons

I'LL NEVER FORGET THE DAY in 1986 when I walked into a dressing room at the Royal Shakespeare Theatre in Stratford to meet one of the most famous people ever to be born on the Isle of Wight. It was for my showbiz column. I was excited and can still vividly remember my first doorway view of Jeremy Irons. It was an uncanny feeling. He seemed to have a visible aura all around him. I had not experienced this before. There was no hint of self-importance and he made me so welcome.

There were some great memories of his early life on a small island. Horse riding on the downs, his acting debut at a small Ryde prep school, watching his father race around St Helens Harbour in his scow dingy, steam train rides and his dreams of becoming a vet.

Jeremy loved boats from an early age and his father, Paul, was one of the founder members of the Brading Haven Yacht Club. His answer to my question of when had he last visited the Isle of Wight involved a sailing story and his wife, famous actress Sinead Cusack.

"A few years ago we sailed from Southsea in an enterprise dingy and landed illegally at Osborne Bay and had a picnic. Then we sailed on to Seaview, which was near my old home at St Helens."

One of my favourite stories from that first interview with Jeremy was that when he left Sherborne School he had no positive plans for his future but had thought about the theatre because of his love of actors biographies. In fact, he actually became a social worker in Peckham. To make his money up he took up busking.

"I used to cycle up to Leicester Square in the evenings, with my guitar on my back, and earn what seemed an enormous amount, like £7 in half an hour."

A few years down the line, some of those London moviegoers who threw money into his cap may well have queued to see his movies like *The French Lieutenant's Woman*, *The Mission*, *Die Hard: With A Vengeance* and *Betrayal*.

Later, in 1999, I was due to interview Jeremy again. This time for my Isle of Wight Radio chat show. I had a very useful contact at London's Langham Hotel and she loved it when I took famous stars there to be interviewed.

I arrived early for my noon interview. I sat in the foyer so as not to miss him, having set up my equipment in a downstairs room. I watched every person arrive for over two hours but Jeremy wasn't among them. Mobile phones and texts were yet to really break big. In the end I went out for a breath of fresh air and, apparently, missed the tannoy message for me to tell me that Jeremy had been delayed at his dentist. He'd come into London on his motorbike.

I got home a few hours later to find several messages on my answer phone with regard to the delays. Sadly, it would have been possible later in the afternoon.

New arrangements were made for me to interview him at the Theatre Royal, Haymarket, where he was meeting many young students for an afternoon session on acting. I sat in the audience and it was so emotional. I remember a young guy doing a speech from a Shakespeare play and Jeremy rushing on stage to congratulate him with a huge hug. It brought the house down.

After the session we moved to the top of the theatre and he gave me a superb hour-long interview. When we walked out together there were still people waiting at the stage door to meet him and he had time for them all. It was an inspirational moment.

CHAPTER 58

Jerry Springer

Amy and Jerry

AMY BIRD IS A YOUNG LADY who should have made the big time. She's such a talented, all-round performer with a real flair for comedy. I have written about her for many years in local papers. Thankfully, a few pantomime producers realised she would be an asset to their shows – and so it proved. When I was invited to see her play Peter Pan, at the New Wimbledon Theatre, it led to a major interview I just didn't expect. When I went backstage after the show she had hinted I might get a surprise.

After I'd interviewed Amy, she disappeared and came back with the one and only Jerry Springer. He was one of the stars of the production, playing Captain Hook, and she had talked him, and later Louis Spence, into appearing on my radio show.

Meeting Jerry was a real delight and most unexpected, but I had to admit that I was not a follower of his world famous television shows, although I had seen one or two. He was certainly not offended and put me at ease straight away.

"There's no excuse for it, I apologise. It's a stupid show and everybody knows that, but it's fun to do," admitted Jerry.

Initially, I wanted to be serious because those who watched his very poignant *Who Do You Think You Are?* BBC show saw another side to him. It was such an emotional experience, as he learnt about many of his family being exterminated during the Second World War. His parents had been lucky and left Germany a few days before the war started. They escaped the Holocaust and somehow managed to get to England, where Jerry was subsequently born.

"I lived in Hampstead but was actually born at Highgate Underground Station, as it was late at night and the war was on."

When he was six the family moved to America. Like fellow Brits, Bob Hope, Cary Grant and Charlie Chaplin, he found fame in America. For many years he was in politics and at one time was an aide to Robert Kennedy and in 1970 Jerry ran for Congress, because he was angry about the Vietnam War. Then he became a media newsreader for many years. Eventually he was offered a talk show and it changed his life.

All of a sudden the mood changed. He told me I'd done so well on his famous television show – and I'd asked him to keep it a secret!!

"Amy, has he never told you he was once a woman on my TV show?" said Jerry, trying to keep a straight face.

When we met in 2011 there had been 4,000 of his shows seen worldwide. Jerry is a genuinely modest person and rather played down his fame.

"I think I'm a nice guy with a reasonably good mind but I'm not talented. I've been successful in the world of showbusiness, which is absurd. I'm still busy but I've been very lucky.

"The people in this pantomime are so professional and talented, it's embarrassing. They have trained and just know what to do and have the skill to dance and act. I just stand and yell."

I was keen to find out a little more about *The Jerry Springer Show* and the people they have on it.

"We are only allowed to have outrageous people on the show. If they've got a warm and uplifting story they will send them to another show.

"Their stories must be factual and truthful but they might embellish them a bit and the audience shout out."

With that, I said farewell to Captain Hook and I'd certainly enjoyed my 'Jerry Springer moment'.

CHAPTER 59

Jimmy Cricket

WHEN A SHOWBIZ PHOTOGRAPHER rings you up specifically to tell you not to miss an act destined for the top, you expect something rather special. So I headed for Warner's, Puckpool Park, to see a comic who was completely new to me. His name was Jimmy Cricket. I saw him send 400 people into a state of uncontrollable laughter. This guy was certain to be a star. Within five years he was headlining in his first television series which ran for four seasons and his supporting cast included Rory Bremner, Bob Todd, Jessica Martin, Joan Sims and Brian Conley.

We next met two years later at Sandown Pavilion, where he was booked for a major summer season. When I interviewed him for the first time at the holiday centre he made you feel like an old friend. By the end of his Sandown run we had become old friends and both had children of around the same age. The day the Cricket family came to Sunday tea was unforgettable.

They arrived in Jimmy's brand new top-of-the-range Ford car and I was envious when he parked it next to my Escort. Excited with his new acquisition, Jimmy suggested we go to the nearby Rookley Country Park in his Granada. We all sat in Jimmy's pride and joy but it wouldn't start. It had run out of petrol. My neighbour loaned us a can and said "come 'ere, come 'ere." I had to drive to the nearest garage to get Jimmy on the road.

We eventually arrived at the country park and as we walked away Jimmy's wife, the lovely May, shouted "where's Frank?" Their young son was missing. It all ended happily. Jimmy had locked his new motor and left his son right up in the back compartment trying to get out.

In the early days of my radio show it was live on a Saturday night. On one occasion I was due to go and pick Jimmy up to bring him to the studio. He was nowhere to be found. I rang the studio and he answered the phone.

Ryde-based scriptwriter Raymond Allen, who wrote *Some Mothers Do 'Ave 'Em*, which unleashed Frank Spencer to the world, wanted to meet Jimmy. I arranged this and they have been close friends ever since. Raymond, in fact, wrote some of the comedy sketches in Jimmy's television series.

One of Raymond's most embarrassing moments was having to join Jimmy on the local Dotto Train. The comedian sat behind the driver and was in his element waving to everyone and Raymond, in his home town, was a little embarrassed, sat at the back with nowhere to hide.

During Jimmy's summer season on the Isle of Wight he did me one real favour. I was such a fan of Tony Hancock, who I'd seen twice live at the Kings, Southsea, and he introduced me to his agent, Phyllis Rounce, (pictured) who had discovered the comic genius.

Jimmy Cricket was another former Butlin's Redcoat to make the big time and he admitted what we all knew.

"Us Redcoats used to stand in the wings and write down all the gags from the visits of the star comedians. We then had our own act at the end of the summer."

Many years later it went full circle. His gags were jotted down by ambitious young performers.

Jimmy has a lot to thank holiday centres for. He was spotted in one by a TV talent scout which led directly to *Search For A Star*. They had certainly found one.

Phyllis with Jimmy

CHAPTER 60

Keith Harris

"I DON'T SUPPOSE you've ever met a real star before, have you, John?," enquired Orville, when I ventured backstage at the Kings Theatre, Southsea. Cuddles said even less, but it was much more predictable:" I hate that duck." Just keeping a wary eye on both of them was a guy called Keith Harris.

Over the years, the likeable Keith was a butt of various jokes and mickey takes. He certainly made the most of these and definitely had the last laugh because he earned a fortune merely putting his hand up the bum of a green duck. In the latter days of his successful career he almost had it all done for him. Clever mechanics meant the duck could make his own entrances and talk to the audience, with Keith just off stage. It worked a treat.

I was lucky enough to see five Keith Harris pantomimes at the Fernham Hall, Fareham, and they brought a new era of Christmas productions to this Hampshire theatre. He certainly knew how to entertain children. Away from his panto and summer seasons, Keith and his pals also had a show for a more mature audience. The late night punters loved it.

Ironically, Keith began his showbiz career in the role of the dummy. At the age of nine he joined his father to form a comedy act that included sitting on dad's knee, pretending to be a wooden doll. Since then he'd emerged into the standing up role to become Britain's most famous ventriloquist since Peter Brough and Archie Andrews.

Working with animals could have meant a whole lot more to Keith Harris – with not one able to answer back. The school careers officer misunderstood his future plans and had him down to be a vet. It was just as well you know who was asleep in the corner. The exhaustion of stardom, no doubt.

In the early days of his showbiz career it was certainly not the star dressing room. He made all his own puppets and dolls and kept an eye on the star vents like Arthur Worsley and Dennis Spicer. Keith reflected on those days.

"Ventriloquism is an old fashioned thing and a dying art, so I saw what was going on in the country and used all my theatre experience to go slightly backwards and become a success."

He perfected the well-groomed image, decided to be his natural self and aimed to be on the same level as those he was entertaining. It set him up for stardom with more than a little help from a duck and a monkey.

Keith became just more than a run-of-the-mill ventriloquist. He quickly realised two hours of Orville was too boring. Hence the *Keith Harris Show* and a couple of hours of varied fare.

In an early '80s television series some critics described him as being a little rude. "It was the work of eight top scriptwriters and you should have seen the stuff we had to cut out," said Keith.

When *The Sun* printed a story about the rude show the viewing figures soared by three million.

Once when the show was being filmed in Birmingham he was asked by the matron of the biggest children's hospital in the city, if he and Orville could pay them a visit. "As long as Orville can come, it doesn't matter about you," stressed the matron. In the end they both made it.

As I left the Kings Theatre, I asked Orville about the stories of Keith and his late-night parties. "He's too old for all that now," said the duck.

CHAPTER 61

Mike Reid

MIKE REID HAD REFUSED all interviews for almost four years – and I knew the reason why. "If you want to talk about my showbusiness career, that's okay, but if it's my family life you can **** off", was his honest opening greeting.

I have always considered a star's private life to be just that. Mike knew this – and we quickly became mates over a lemonade and orange juice. On another occasion he had minders with him but told them to disappear.

If Mike hadn't slipped a disc it's highly unlikely we would ever have heard of him. Before finding fame as a comedian, he was a mime artist, but mime acts never top theatre bills or get prime television slots. As for his famous voice that blew his disguise anywhere in Britain, in his original act he only ever said "good evening" and "goodnight." Years later they were queuing up to book him for voice-overs.

Mike was late for a lunchtime gig at the Reform Club, Kentish Town and was in the middle of humping all of his equipment up the stairs. With a Vox speaker, weighing over one cwt, under his arm, and a hefty amplifier under the other he collapsed in a heap. Rumour suggests he never mimed his words as he fell down.

During his stay in hospital, he was told to change his act or get out of the business. He took the advice and Mike Reid, comedian, was born and the rest has been well documented and he ended up entertaining millions as Frank Butcher in *EastEnders*.

During his mime act days he'd also worked as a stunt man in movies and TV series. His credits included *The Saint, The Avengers, Champions* and *The Baron*.

Mike was a self-confessed workaholic. I had proof of this in 1993 during one of my later interviews with him. He drove to the Isle of Wight early in the morning, had a round of golf at Osborne House, performed an afternoon cabaret at the Westland's Aerospace Club, went off to an hotel for three hours sleep, set his alarm to wake up for our interview, did another evening cabaret show, then drove to London from the midnight car ferry to sleep in his *EastEnders* dressing room ready for the day's shooting.

"I am tired but not complaining. There are 160,000 actors out of work at any one time. Some people say I should go out and get a proper job. I work a minimum of 16 hours a day and more often it's nearer 22."

Despite his regular appearances in *EastEnders* he could never forget he was a comedian. It was in his blood and he just loved entertaining.

"If I won a million pounds I'd still go out and work as a comedian. I love the smell and the touch of an audience."

Personally, I admired Mike Reid so much. In his life he suffered more sadness than most but still came back fighting. That was such an enviable attitude. I don't know how he coped with everything.

On the last occasion we ever met he told me: "It's just in me to fight back. I'll never be beaten by anything. Life in general just won't beat me. Some people get hit on the head, go down and stay down. They say they've had enough and then just tick over. I won't stand for that, I'm proud to say."

CHAPTER 62

Nigel Havers

NIGEL HAVERS WAS TOURING Britain in the play Rebecca and it was all arranged for me to visit him in Cardiff to promote his forthcoming visit to the Mayflower, Southampton. From the Isle of Wight to the city's New Theatre was at least a 10-hour round trip by ferry and train. The plan was to interview him between the matinee and the evening performance. I'd had a meal in a nearby restaurant and headed for the stage door, where they are always so helpful. Just minutes after the curtain came down a voice on the tannoy announced that Mr Havers taxi was waiting outside the theatre. Down rushed Nigel and when he spotted me he said: "Christ, I forgot you were coming. I'm in a hurry but can spare you just 10 minutes."

We quickly headed to his dressing room and it took me about five minutes to set up. While this was happening, I suddenly had a thought. I'd interviewed him a couple of years earlier in Brighton about the early days of his career and might be able to get away with it. I started the radio interview and did not mention his early days at all. I picked up on the last two years, the current tour of *Rebecca* and his future plans. When I got back home I edited the two interviews together and it made around 25 minutes, which was the perfect length to slot into my two-hour chat show. No one realised the first half of the interview was in Brighton and the second half in Cardiff, with two years in between. Thankfully, neither of us had a cold at either interview, otherwise it couldn't have been done.

What I particularly like about Nigel Havers is the way he challenges himself to broaden his career. It's hard to believe it all began in the quaint radio series *Mrs Dale's Diary*. Since then, to name but a few, there's been *Chariots Of Fire*, *The Charmer*, Lewis Archer in *Coronation Street*, *Little Britain*, *Celebrity Carry On Barging*, *Benidorm*, *I'm A Celebrity... Get Me Out Of Here*, *Downton Abbey* and scary pantomime baddie roles. I can also remember enjoying the first *The Afternoon Play* he produced on television. It gave him great personal satisfaction.

"I think I'm obsessed with my job and I'm always looking for new ideas," said Nigel. When I first met him it was after a matinee performance of *Art*, at the Theatre Royal, Brighton. An hour or so earlier, on a snowy Sussex afternoon, you could clearly hear the sighs of delight when Nigel first walked on stage. He suggested they were all around 85. There were a few shades of grey on view in the capacity audience.

At that particular time he had an ambition to play a real East End villain – and to become Lord Mayor of London. I don't think the latter was a realistic dream. He just clearly didn't like Ken Livingstone or his newly introduced congestion charges.

Nigel has always had a great affection for radio. In the early days of his career he was a researcher for Jimmy Young's innovative Radio 2 current affairs programme.

"I loved working for Jimmy Young. He was one of the great radio men of all time," enthused Nigel, who was clearly too young, if you'll pardon the pun, to remember Jimmy as a pop star.

Nigel's father was a QC but he never had any ambition to follow that career path. He was at prep school when he decided to be an actor and will be eternally grateful to the master who encouraged him.

Richard Todd

WHEN I WAS A YOUNG SCHOOLBOY my late father, Roy, had a friend who was the cinema projectionist at Osborne House, Queen Victoria's former home, part of which formed a convalescent wing for injured officers and service personnel. Dad had a GB Bell and Howell sound projector at home and we viewed the movies the previous evening to make sure they were in perfect condition for the officers to watch. Sometimes I played the records before and after the show. It meant I grew up watching some amazing movies and I loved our major stars like Richard Todd. Many years later I had the chance to interview him.

We met backstage at the Theatre Royal, Windsor. What a perfect gentleman he was. He even borrowed the dressing room of another actor, as his own had the noisy sound of water pipes, not ideal for a radio recording.

There were certain things I just had to ask him about. *The Hasty Heart*, with Hollywood stars Ronald Reagan and Patricia Neal, was the perfect start. What was the man who went on the become the American President really like?

"He was extremely nice and so kind to me, as it was only my second picture and he was an established star. He always had us in fits of laughter with his great sense of fun. When he became President people seemed to want to decry his role as a movie actor, but he was actually darned good.

"When we were filming it was very icy and I had a few hairy moments with my old car. Ronnie found out about this and picked me up every day in his chauffeured limousine en route from the Savoy Hotel to the film set – and back again. We became such close friends."

Richard was so surprised that even before *The Hasty Heart* came out, Alfred Hitchcock had signed him for his *Stage Fright* movie, alongside Jane Wyman, Marlene Dietrich and Michael Wilding. He loved working with the great director.

When *The Hasty Heart* did come out, Richard was a Golden Globe winner and Oscar-nominated. Among his other great memories was making a movie with Bette Davis and walking past a London cinema and seeing in huge letters simply, 'Richard Todd In *The Yangtse Incident*.'

The Dam Busters movie just had to come up. I also loved the theme tune and it was the first 78rpm record my parents ever bought me. Richard was so proud of that movie and never tired of talking about it.

"Once when I was in the 20th Century Fox Studio in America I got the movie in from Canada to show the great Darryl Zanuck. He loved it and at the end he actually shouted out across the room 'Gee that's a great movie. Is that a true story?' When I told him it was, he added: 'Why the hell doesn't it say so?' He just didn't believe it had really happened."

For some reason, which he kept to himself, he did not want to talk about *The Long, The Short And The Tall*. All he would say was: "I hated it immensely."

Richard made three films for Walt Disney and initially turned down the chance to play Robin Hood. Despite pressure from his agent, he still would not change his mind. Then Disney invited him to lunch and would not take no for an answer. It was a huge hit.

"What I didn't like were the bloody horses. In Hollywood, where so many great westerns have been made, they have trained horses for everything. Some can fall and others can bite, rear-up or kick. I made pictures with their horses. The ones in Robin Hood were old screws and on the way to the knacker's yard."

CHAPTER 64

Shane Richie

WHEN I FIRST SAW SHANE RICHIE, he was a Pontin's Bluecoat at Little Canada Holiday Centre, on the Isle of Wight. I admired his enthusiasm but didn't foresee such a brilliant future ahead. I actually saw him perform a rather strange act as Luke Skywalker, when he supported Lenny Henry at a Sunday concert at Sandown Pavilion. I'm still not quite sure he ever knew what he was actually trying to do on that night.

His adventures at the Wootton holiday centre, amidst the totem pole, unfortunate rambles with campers and quite a few notches on his chalet door, were well chronicled in his brilliant autobiography, *From Rags To Richie*. Among his staff, when he became entertainment's manager, was a guy called Ron Sheppard, who has gone on to be Britain's most married man.

Pontin's used Shane's amazing story as a slogan for their recruitment drive for new camp entertainers. It read: 'From Pontin's to the London Palladium in four years.'

Ironically, despite his new found fame, I saw him struggle with an ageing audience in a 1992 end-of-season star cabaret night at the Whitecliff Bay Holiday Centre. He was too quick and clever for the invited guests. I thought he was superb and, by then, expected him to go on to great things.

I could never have imagined that a few years later I would see him give the greatest portrayal of Scrooge that I have ever seen on a stage. The setting was the giant Mayflower Theatre, in Southampton, and it was in the Leslie Bricusse musical.

I gave him a rave review in *The Stage* and his *EastEnders* mate Barbara Windsor cheekily asked him if he'd slept with me to get such a wonderful critique.

What I like about Shane, Brian Conley, Bradley Walsh and Joe Pasquale is that they always still remember their roots and the people they met at the very beginning of their careers in holiday centre entertainment.

I have enjoyed all their successes. I even watched TV game shows that Shane hosted, for pleasure and not work. I also liked him in the comeback series of *Minder* and he followed this with some other great TV dramas. He's also starred in some top West End musicals and, of course, become famous as a certain Alfie Moon.

Going back to his roots, I love the story of how he lied about his age to get an audition for Pontin's. He should have been 18 but was actually only just 15.

"I told them I was interested in comedy, singing, acting and dancing. They gave me a job as a sports organiser. When I should have been taking my school exams I was running donkey derbies and *It's A Knockout* camp events."

In those days he was earning around £28 a week. A few years later he went back as one of Pontin's star cabaret acts and probably earned much more in 50 minutes than he previously got paid for a whole summer season.

Shane has always appreciated the television opportunities generously created for him by such respected pros as Jimmy Tarbuck and Des O'Connor. No doubt he has now helped budding youngsters hoping to follow him.

He's one of those famous people who is always pleased to see you – and it's a real genuine warmth. The last time we caught up was with his *EastEnders* co-star Jesse Wallace. I told her things about Shane she knew nothing about, in their joint interview. It worked a treat! Apparently, he even liked my book on pop stars.

CHAPTER 65

Brenda Blethyn

WHEN I MET UP with Brenda Blethyn in Eastbourne, she was touring in the *Glass Menagerie*. Our interview was to pre-promote her forthcoming visit to Chichester, to appear in the show. We both had a surprise for each other. She had great stories about movie icons like Robert Redford and actually doubled our time together, as she was enjoying it so much. I was flattered and glad I had spent some time in finding out her favourite records by Alma Cogan, Bobby Darin and Doris Day, which she didn't expect.

What an amazing story and it all began not long after she was born. I wanted to find out more about her extra finger.

"Yes, I was born with an extra finger. The doctor cut if off and told my mother I was going to be an actress. If he'd known I was going to be a typist he might have kept it on and I could have typed much faster," said Brenda.

In fact, she became a typist before she had even thought about acting and revealed the story.

"I was a typist for British Rail and our local am dram group were desperate because one of their members was sick. I told them I couldn't do anything like that. It was only one line and they talked me into it. I loved it from that time and began appearing in amateur productions."

A few years later she was acting in movies with Michael Caine, Kris Kristofferson, Brad Pitt, Donald Sutherland and John Hurt.

Brenda was spotted working in amateur productions in the Chichester area. A local theatre director, who was very impressed, told her she should train to be a professional. Eventually, she took his advice and went to the Guildford School of Acting, alongside other hopefuls like Celia Imrie and Bill Nighy. When she left, powerful actor John Judd, who was in *Scum*, recommended her to the Bubble Theatre Company and her professional career was up and running.

When she was at the National Theatre playing small parts, Kate Nelligan, one of the stars, left and the staff director was convinced Brenda could take her place and even managed to persuade Peter Hall. A new British star was in the making.

I first discovered Brenda in the television series *Outside Edge*, with Robert Dawes playing her domineering husband Roger Dervish. He made 'Mim' do virtually everything, with not a thank you in sight, although his favourite saying was "love you Mim." He was a far better talker than a cricketer. Sorry skipper!

Secrets And Lies, for which she won six major awards, *Saving Grace*, *Pumpkin*, *Pride And Prejudice* and *Little Voice* were among her great movie successes. I loved the story of when she was preparing to return to England, following a run in a Broadway show.

"I was packing my bags when I had a phone call and they said it was from Robert Redford's office. I didn't believe them at first but then realised it really was. Apparently, he wanted me for his movie A *River Runs Through It*.

"I turned up to meet some of his people and he suddenly appeared. He came running towards me and gave me a huge hug and embrace and told me he was delighted to meet me. I kept saying to myself, 'this is Robert Redford, this is Robert Redford.' I couldn't believe it."

The morning after Brenda was seen in her first major television role, Mike Leigh's *Grown Ups*, one of her neighbours spotted her hanging out the washing.

"Brenda, did Reg and I see you on television last night?" She replied: "You might have done." Then came the unanticipated reply: "We thought it was you but we switched it off!"

CHAPTER 66

Charlie Williams

"WHEN I KNEW I WAS COMING to the Isle of Wight, I wondered whether they would let me in. They might have mistaken me for an illegal immigrant, especially if I arrived by canoe," quipped Charlie Williams, when I first met him in late 1977. He'd popped over for a cabaret one-nighter but came back for several summers at Sandown Pavilion.

Charlie was perfect for a summer show. He would wander up and down the seafront chatting to old ladies, making a fuss of the youngsters and cracking one-liners to keep the guys amused. It was a shrewd ploy because many of them ended up going to his end of the pier show. On stage he could get away with things other comedians just wouldn't have risked. The 'ole flowers' in the audience loved every minute.

I always remember inviting Charlie to appear live on my Sunday lunchtime chat show. He asked if I could pick him up from the house in Brading, where he was stopping. I allowed myself plenty of time but went around the block several times because I couldn't find him. He was stood on a very high bank and I just couldn't spot him from the car. Eventually I found him and the show was due to start in 20 minutes and we were five miles away. It was a case of hold on tight Charlie. We made it while the news was on. He told the listeners: "I saw John keep coming around the block and I wondered what was going on. I saw him every time."

Charlie had initially made the national headlines as a black, former Doncaster Rovers footballer who made it big on *The Comedians*. The fans loved him and his Yorkshire accent and he became one of the hottest comics in British showbiz. He also became a huge hit fronting *The Golden Shot*.

Despite his amazing success on television it was not his first love.

He told me: "It's not really my media. I don't want the cameras. Cabaret and summer seasons are my scene. I thrive on live audiences and love people."

Incidentally, when Charlie did a television commercial for Yorkshire Bitter, which was never shown in his home county, for an obvious reason, their national sales figures rose by nearly 40 percent.

My favourite Charlie Williams story is not a gag – and his lovely wife Janice had little to laugh about. They were staying in a posh hotel and his wife was having a relaxing bath when the fire alarm went off.

"We'd had some champagne with friends to celebrate our wedding and we went back to our hotel to unwind. It was our honeymoon night. Janice said she wanted a bath so I told her I would read the paper. Then the fire alarm went off and I thought it must be a practice. Then I realised it was for real. I quickly grabbed my watch, money and car keys and left Janice in the bath and ran for it. I did grab a spare pair of knickers and her dressing gown. She did need them as we had to cross the street to the hotel opposite."

Charlie Williams was great company and he once told me what a wise old Barbadian, who just happened to be his dad, had told him: "If a man has a friend, he's a rich man. If that's the case, I'm a very wealthy man!" said Charlie.

CHAPTER 67

Tony Adams

I FIRST ENCOUNTERED Tony Adams back in the spring of 1985 when I got a message that *Crossroads'* Adam Chance was staying on a boat called *Sylvia* V in a Cowes river. I had to scramble over a couple of other boats to reach him and it was well worth the effort.

It was no great surprise to find him on the Isle of Wight. His first Cowes Week had been back in 1950. Surely, he must have been so young at the time! It had been a busy day for him after filming the famous soap in Birmingham. He'd grabbed a few hours sleep, left the city at 4.15am and caught the ferry to Cowes three hours later. It must have seemed another world from John Latchford, Nicola Freeman and Sid Hooper.

Tony had such a famous face at that time and even before Adam Chance the ladies swooned at his Doctor Bywaters character in *General Hospital*. In the local Cowes supermarket, he was only buying a few provisions but was stopped nine times for his autograph. Worse was to follow. As he left the store he was mobbed by 40 children.

"Normally I like meeting fans but I had an urgent appointment and could not stop to sign all those autographs. I felt terrible about it and some of the kids were rude to me," said Tony.

Many expected Tony to be born with a plaice in one hand and a bottle of gin in the other. At the time his mother was a trawler skipper on the Irish Sea – and two weeks overdue. Tony had been in love with the sea ever since.

His mother was an incredible lady. She played hockey and ice hockey for England, had a golf handicap of four, won cups for swimming and diving, was a county tennis player, the first woman to win the King's Cup aeroplane race and even explored the Amazon for the *Daily Express*.

When his mother died in 1984, at the age of 85, he brought her ashes back to the Solent and scattered them in the water.

"I also threw in a vodka and martini at the same time. That's what she would have wanted to go with her," revealed Tony. Her dream was for him to be Admiral Adams but there weren't too many of them at Italia Conti.

As a youngster he trained as a dancer and worked with the Festival Ballet and when he came to the local boatyard he would perform his bar warm-ups every morning. The only music was the wolf whistles from the workmen.

Long before *Crossroads* and its 16 million viewers, he appeared in hit stage shows like *Mame*, *Sail Away* and *West Side Story*. He, of course, made his name through soap operas.

"They appeal to me. I'm not your run-of-the-mill actor with an ambition to play Hamlet at the National. My derivation of the word success is to be in constant work. In my business 80 per cent of actors are always out of work. I want to get up every morning and know I have a job."

Tony may not have played Hamlet for the RSC but he did join Christopher Biggins and Jason Donovan in *Chitty Chitty Bang Bang* at the London Palladium.

The last time I saw Tony was in a Southsea panto and he was swanking with his new *Crossroads* phone theme and he played it on air and couldn't stop it. It proved great radio – and Tony Hatch would have been delighted.

CHAPTER 68

Uri Geller

LIKE MILLIONS OF OTHERS, I was enthralled when I first saw Uri Geller on television. I could never quite make up my mind as to whether it was a con or that he really had unique powers. Unexpectedly, my big chance came to find out. An interview was arranged for me in the unlikely surroundings of a Soho pub called The Blue Posts. Being of a certain age, that part of London still held a certain mystique for me – as did Uri.

I sat in the downstairs bar, waiting for the great man to arrive. All of a sudden he swept in through the door, shook my hand and gave me the once over with those piercing eyes. Within five minutes he had bought me a Coke and bent a spoon right in front of me. Even the drinkers put down their glasses to give him a round of applause. What a start!

They suggested the upstairs bar would be the ideal location for our radio interview, as it was closed on that afternoon. The young barmaid took us up and Uri noticed the clock on the wall was not working and asked her how long it had been out of action for. She had been there for four years and it had not been working in that time. Now this really was going to test Mr Geller. He stood on a chair, got right in front of the clock, uttered a few words and waved his hands in front of the face. I thought nothing more about this and set up my equipment. Uri gave me a 30-minute interview and at the end, I casually glanced at the clock and realised it had been going for the full length of our chat. Suddenly, any doubts I had about Uri Geller disappeared.

That was not the end of the story. In our recorded interview, he asked any listeners who had stopped clocks to go and get them and a few minutes later he told them just what to do, with a few special words. Remember this was a pre-recorded interview. When we played it live on air people phoned in to say their broken clocks had suddenly started to work again. It was so eerie. Believe it or not, a few months later I repeated the interview and people still rang in to say their clocks had started again.

I found Uri's family history fascinating. His mother and father had met and married in Hungary and then fled to Israel, where his father fought for the British Army, in the Jewish Brigade, against Rommel in North Africa. Then Uri took me completely by surprise.

"I have something very sad to tell you and I only found out about it recently. My father actually forced my mother to have eight abortions, so I am really the ninth child," revealed Uri. Not surprisingly, she later divorced him.

Uri, who was in the Israeli Army for a while, also worked as an export manager and a male model. Don't tell anyone, but he did model underwear. During his school days he'd been bullied because of his supernatural feats, which included spoon and fork bending and his ability to advance a clock with his special powers. He was called either a magician, a freak or miracle worker.

In 1969 he was engaged to perform a key bending demonstration, which eventually led to him performing for generals and judges.

"My life really changed when I performed for Golda Meir, the Prime Minister of Israel, where I also did some mind reading. When Golda was asked what did she predict for the future of her country, she replied: 'Don't ask me, ask Uri Geller!' That went around the world very quickly and completely changed my life."

Uri Geller with John holding the bent spoon

CHAPTER 69

Tom O'Connor

IT'S BEEN SUCH A PLEASURE to have made so many good friends over the past 45 years and Tom O'Connor and his lovely wife Pat, his constant travelling companion, fall into this category. They have always found time to see me and we have often met up socially, when they have been in the area for one-nighters. Tom had a summer season at Sandown Pavilion and has been a regular visitor to our local Warner Holiday Centres. The last time I met him, in 2015, he told me he had 32 cruises booked for the following year. I thought I was a workaholic! The Americans lapped up his gentle, clean and reflective humour.

When Isle of Wight Radio went from medium wave to FM, I was asked who I could get to join our fun day and meet the listeners. As Tom was working at a Warner's Centre the night before, he seemed the perfect choice. He was in great form and the crowd loved him. I interviewed him live on-air during my Sunday show. I also had, what I thought was a clever idea, and Tom was up for it. He did me a voicer, in other words, a free plug for my chat show, and he mentioned all the game shows he had hosted, to become a world record-holder.

I used to get very frustrated when I saw several cabaret comedians using a lot of Tom's act. I know it's always happened. Thankfully, some of those who nicked them did not quite have his delivery style or 32 cruises in the book.

I'll always remember the first time I met Tom. It was back in 1980 and he recalled a great story and it formed the opening paragraph to the first article I ever wrote on him. It was as follows:

'Around the mid '60s, Tom O'Connor's bank balance could not even run to the cost of a school dinner. That rags to riches showbiz cliché is just about worn out. In Tom's case, it really was 2/8d to international stardom.'

It's been well publicised that he was a schoolteacher for 13 years. When Pat, who had also been a teacher, was having their third child he was earning £9 a week.

"We were desperate for cash and I became a semi-pro entertainer by necessity. I began as a country singer but soon realised comedians could earn more money," reflected Tom. While at teacher training college he had written and run a few revues. His forte at that time was parodies like Big Fred Mac, based on Jimmy Dean's Big Bad John.

Opportunity Knocks was his big break. He was in six consecutive shows and later in the year was invited back for the All Winners Show. Hughie Green tempted Lord Delfont to sit in a special box and he was particularly impressed with Tom. The impresario said to officials from Thames Television: "Who has got this fella?" They lied and answered "We have." The outcome was *Wednesday At Eight* and stardom.

Back to our first-ever meeting in 1980. Tom finished his 70-minute cabaret spot at 12.10am and then 35 minutes later caught the last ferry home to head to London for a lunchtime show. Then he drove on to Hereford for an evening gig.

Every Christmas my family looked forward to Tom's Christmas card. It was always full of pictures of his family, with more additions every year.

On one occasion, I really felt sorry for Tom and Pat. There was no room available to stay at the cabaret venue and they were given a bedroom at a local pub. I interviewed him there and left in a hurry, quickly followed by them. They drove back to their Berkshire home instead.

CHAPTER 70

Dave Allen

IN SEPTEMBER 2000, I was invited to the evening press launch of Richard Stone's autobiography, *You Should Have Been In Last Night*, at the Green Room Club in London. There were famous stars everywhere including David Jason, June Whitfield, Andrew Sachs and Dave Allen. Even the national photographers came over to see if I knew who was who.

I had got to know Richard in the previous year or so and was delighted to have had him on my radio show. I invited him back for a second time to talk about his new book. I also asked if he thought someone famous might talk to me at the London launch – and I know he was keen on this idea.

After so many years of interviewing, I had got a sense of when to ask or when to leave alone. I saw David Jason arrive and did not go near him for around 15 minutes. Then I politely asked if he could do a short interview about Richard to help plug the book. He was very non-committal and said he might but was not very helpful in any way. I quickly disappeared. When Dave Allen walked in, I let him settle for a while and then casually asked him the same question. I also explained to him, as I did to David, that the interview equipment was all set up in a downstairs room.

"Let's go down and do it straight away," said a very happy and enthusiastic Dave Allen. In the end we talked for about 15 minutes about Richard and his own career.

When I went back upstairs I politely told David Jason that Dave Allen had just given me a few minutes and would he like to add a few words. I remember his reply to this day: "You're too late now, you've missed your chance." I was very disappointed, but continued to watch the superb acting talents of Jason in his hit television shows.

Ironically, the next time I met Dave Allen was just a couple of weeks later. It was the last place we would have chosen – and much too quickly. It was at the Isle of Wight funeral service for Richard Stone, who had died a few days after the book launch. We all knew he was ill but it was sooner than expected. I had the feeling Richard somehow had managed to hold on until after the launch. I walked with Dave from the Seaview church to Richard and Sara's house for the wake. Sadly, Dave Allen died in 2005.

On a happier note, that London interview was a gem and he gave me some fantastic stories. Like the time he was booked on the most famous television show in the world, America's *Ed Sullivan Show*, on an Ascension Sunday. They hated his comedy routine, about death, coffins, burial and the wake and would not let him appear on the big televised evening show. So he came back home and continued to be Dave Allen, the comic we all loved.

Once at the Savoy Hotel, London, he was banned from jokes about religion, the English, the Irish, blacks and politics. He told me: "There was nothing left of my act. So I told the audience I was banned from telling all these stories and then promptly did them."

Initially, Dave had television success in Australia with his own shows, thanks to Sophie Tucker, who suggested to an Aussie agent that he should tour Down Under. In Britain, many years later, he first found fame on the Val Doonican show, for 13 weeks. He was on his best behaviour, too.

Finally he revealed his great love and respect for Richard Stone, whom he'd known for 43 years. I know the feeling was mutual.

CHAPTER 71

Des O'Connor

DES O'CONNOR WAS BOOKED for a 1987 Sunday Concert at Sandown Pavilion and it was completely sold-out. I went through the official channels to try and arrange an interview but had no success at all, via his agent or management. I went down to catch the soundcheck and discovered his road manager was none other than my good friend Anthony Bishop. I told him how sorry I was not that I had not been allowed to interview Des. Suddenly, I sensed there might be some hope.

"Come backstage after the show and in the meantime I'll have a chat with Des," said Anthony, always the perfect gentleman.

My luck was in and Des gave me a great interview and it proved to be the first of several, over the following years. This was the first time I'd ever seen Des live and I was completely stunned by the brilliance of his performance. I became an instant fan long before the interval of his real one-man show. The next morning I sent a rave review to *The Stage* – and it was printed.

"I just wish the press would come and see me. Then they would know what I am trying to do for the public. They just say I can't sing and I'm not funny. With a live crowd it's a bit of magic.

"People take the trouble to drive cars, catch buses or trains to see me perform, so I don't hide in the dressing room for 90 minutes and just turn up for the last half hour. That's stealing. I get in for nothing," said Des.

I have met so many young stars, particularly comedians, who have praised Des for giving them a chance on his great television series.

A few years later I took Jack Douglas, who worked as a partner to Des for many years, to Warner's Bembridge Coast Hotel to see him perform. Afterwards we were invited to his fabulous suite overlooking the sea. It was remarkable. We stayed for over an hour and Des and Jack both remembered routines they had done together many years earlier. It was like a private midnight cabaret.

Des invited me to the Bournemouth Pavilion a few days later to interview him. His stay at Bembridge had been rather hectic and there had been no time. I did finally achieve a Des O'Connor hat-trick when I went to his Surrey home to pre-record a 45-minute interview to promote a forthcoming show. What a day that was as we sat and ate chocolate cakes.

"John before you go I know you would like to see my snooker room because you love memorabilia," suggested Des. I could barely wait.

What a surprise! His numerous gold discs were all around the walls. Morecambe and Wise would have had a field day. There were wonderful posters, including his 1958 British tour with Buddy Holly – and a guitar given to him by the late rock 'n' roll legend.

Des went on to even more television series and on *Today With Des And Mel* he again introduced some brilliant young comics. When Bradley Walsh came on live it was a show to treasure – and after being on he kept looking through the window.

The *Des O'Connor Tonight* series was live for many years until three guys proved more than a handful. They were, of course, Freddie Starr, Oliver Reed and Stan Boardman. Enough said!! They pre-recorded soon after that.

CHAPTER 72

Geoffrey Hughes

OVER THE YEARS, I have enjoyed many tip-offs that have led to wonderful interviews and, in some cases, the start of friendships. I was told by an Isle of Wight sailing club that actor Geoffrey Hughes kept his boat in their anchorage and came down every few weeks. I left a letter addressed to him. I could so easily have written on it Eddie Yeats, Onslow, Twiggy or Vernon Scripps and it would have still reached him. Eventually he moved to the Island and one day left me a message at my home, agreeing to an interview.

I know the friendly people at Isle of Wight Lavender put in a good word for me. This was one of Geoff's favourite places and not far from his own property. The lane to his home was not car-friendly and he suggested we meet at the lavender farm. I wondered if he'd arrive on his quad bike. There were local stories around that he was a kind of off-road Stirling Moss.

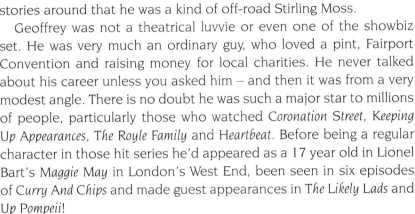

Geoffrey was not a theatrical luvvie or even one of the showbiz set. He was very much an ordinary guy, who loved a pint, Fairport Convention and raising money for local charities. He never talked about his career unless you asked him – and then it was from a very modest angle. There is no doubt he was such a major star to millions of people, particularly those who watched *Coronation Street*, *Keeping Up Appearances*, *The Royle Family* and *Heartbeat*. Before being a regular character in those hit series he'd appeared as a 17 year old in Lionel Bart's *Maggie May* in London's West End, been seen in six episodes of *Curry And Chips* and made guest appearances in *The Likely Lads* and *Up Pompeii*!

For 17 years I ran the Isle of Wight Amateur Theatre Awards, which meant seeing about 50 shows a year and then choosing the nominations and hosting the evening. I'll never forget the first time Geoff came as a surprise guest to present the awards. I'd recorded four famous TV themes to introduce our mystery star. The music had barely gone from *Coronation Street* into *Keeping Up Appearances* when the roar went up and drowned out the music from *The Royle Family* and *Heartbeat*.

The Isle of Wight people instantly took to Geoffrey Hughes and he readily did so much for charity. Everything from opening shows to switching on Christmas lights. He also made so many local friends who knew nothing about showbusiness – and he loved that. One of his closest pals was a notorious ex-local footballer called Brian Morey, a local pony breeder. They had such fun together.

Geoff loved his new location and did not want to spend 48 weeks of his year on *Heartbeat*. He turned down a telephone number salary to continue in the series or make a surprise comeback in others. He was just happy living with his lovely wife Sue in their dream home and running his own business, Wood End Enterprises, which supplied wood mulch, chips and kindling.

Whilst having a hip replacement in a Southampton Hospital, Geoff met one of his all-time heroes, Jet Harris, from the original Shadows, who also lived on the Isle of Wight. They became instant friends after meeting, unexpectedly, while they smoked outside in their wheelchairs. When they came on my radio show together, Geoff admitted he would have loved to have been in the Shadows and Jet wished he played some of Geoff's television roles.

It was so sad when Geoff died in 2012. There was standing room only at his very emotional funeral, where Heartbeat stars rubbed shoulders with his local pals. He loved Fairport Convention and members of the group played at his funeral. I was privileged just to have known him.

CHAPTER 73

James Earl Jones

CAROLINE WAS USED TO MEETING famous stars from a very early age, as she accompanied me on some interviews. We didn't know it at the time but this was to prove so useful during her chosen career. She was never fazed by star names and since then has worked with so many, as a head of wardrobe. In fact, she asks them if they would talk to her dad. Over the years only one has ever refused. Hollywood movie star James Earl Jones certainly said yes when she asked him – and he was a real star and not a novice from a TV talent show.

I met James when he was working in a West End production of *Driving Miss Daisy*. It was a delight to meet such an icon. I sensed he might be short of time or need a rest before the matinee show. After a few minutes he picked this up and told me not to rush things, as he had plenty of time. He then talked for not far off an hour.

James had proof that he was descended from a family of slaves. There was a problem with his own birth and he was told by his grandmother that his mother almost gave up and was heard to say "it's dead already." Maggie Connolly, the grandmother, shocked her daughter with foul language and cursed her for saying that. This was intended to make her push harder – and it worked.

"This may surprise you but at 6am that day I can remember seeing the light from a kerosene lamp on the stove. It was if I'd been welcomed by the light of life," said James.

He had a real problem with a stammer and from the age of six until he was 14 he was mute and only talked to himself and animals. They certainly responded to the attention he gave them, with no feedback.

"Going to high school changed my life and it was all down to my English teacher, who wrote poetry. He couldn't handle my problem. Somehow he found out I also wrote poetry and he tricked me into reading one of my poems out loud to the class and I had no problem with it."

James Earl Jones with my daughter Caroline

James ended up being the school's champion of public speaking.

During his career James had made over 100 movies. He admitted to have forgotten some and there were others he was delighted to have forgotten. His major ones include *The Great White Hope*, *Conan The Barbarian*, *The Hunt For Red October* and *Cry, The Beloved Country*.

Many people remember him as the voice of Darth Vader in *Star Wars*. When I suggested it had been a part of his life he said "no" and explained why.

"It's a big part of Dave Prowse's life. I was not the character, Dave was the character. He was in there sweating every day. I was just special effects and originally didn't even want my name on the credits."

Just a couple of weeks before interviewing James, I had been at the Croydon home of Dave Prowse and he had so much respect and admiration for James. I gave him a CD of my interview with Dave and he took it back to the States with him.

I did have one final surprise. James had heard that there was a Norwegian rock group called the *James Earl Jones Barbershop Explosion*. I'd managed to find one of their tracks to play within the interview. He was amazed – and quite chuffed.

CHAPTER 74

Reginald Marsh

WHAT ON EARTH could Arthur Sugden, the works manager from *The Plane Makers*, Dave Smith, the one-time *Coronation Street* bookie, Sir Dennis Hodge, from *Terry and June*, and Andrew, Jerry's boss in *The Good Life*, have in common. They were all played by Reginald Marsh, which made him one of the most well-known television faces in Britain.

Reg had been a regular visitor to the Isle of Wight for many years, before he decided to move there permanently. I was tipped off, but it was to be a secret for a little while. I met him for the first time in an hotel opposite the Sandown Pavilion Theatre. We hit it off instantly and over the years became good friends. Initially, my story did not include the fact he was now living locally. He much appreciated my tact and wanted to settle in quietly before the rush to book him to open endless fetes and other events.

Quite quickly Reg got involved with raising funds for the local MENCAP group. He was closely involved with their Haylands Farm project and his son, Adam, was a student there. On one occasion Reg invited me to attend their special Mastermind evening. It was so emotional and the questions were of varying levels to involve everyone. The rivalry was intense and so many wanted to win. There was not a dry eye in the audience of parents and friends. Reg had a real friend in Alan Titchmarsh and he did so much to draw attention to the project. In fact, the first time I met Alan was at Haylands Farm.

On television, Reg cornered the market for bullying buffoons and it all began in *The Good Life*.

He told me at that first interview: "Television is strange. If you have done as much comedy and light entertainment as me, they put an LE against your name. Then other directors and producers don't seem to offer things. I'm not really a comedian and would love more opportunities for straight acting on the box."

After 40 years of acting, Reg finally got asked to play Falstaff in Shakespeare's *Henry IV - Part 1*. It was not on television but for the prestigious Oxford Playhouse Company.

"I never really thought I'd get offered that part while I was still young enough to do it. It was quite a strenuous role to play."

A few years later he played in Ken Hill's original stage version of *The Phantom Of The Opera*, both in the West End and on its world tour.

Other television roles for him included playing Reg Lamont in *Crossroads* and Humphrey Pumphrey, Mildred's brother-in-law, in *George and Mildred*. On the big screen his movies included *Jigsaw*, *Young Winston* and *The Day The Earth Caught Fire*.

I loved talking to him about playing Dave Smith in *Coronation Street*, when almost half the country watched it.

"For 10 years I had an on-screen romance with Elsie Tanner. It was a non-consummated affair and went on till we became too old to think about it.

"When I was on they always gave me good strong storylines. I normally appeared for a couple of months at a time and didn't just prop up the Rovers Return."

This, obviously, was perfect for Reg and gave him the chance to do other things in between.

In the year 2000, I was so thrilled when Reg came on stage to say a few nice things about me at the launch of my first book. Sadly, he died the following year.

Jethro

I FIRST MET JETHRO in the summer of 1991 and the long and the short of it was, he came in live to my Isle of Wight Radio chat show on the same Sunday lunchtime as Kenny Baker, *Star Wars'* R2D2. Amazingly, the Cornish comedian appeared nervous before the show but once he got on air it was a different matter.

Long before he found real fame on the Des O'Connor TV show, Jethro had a cult following and this included fans on the Isle of Wight. Local businessman Colin Caws, who had represented England as a clay pigeon marksman, first met a guy called Geoffrey Rowe, who also enjoyed the sport. They became friends and Colin discovered he also performed as a comedian called Jethro. Hence, as a favour to his friend, who was also the president of the Newport Rotary Club, he appeared for a Ladies Night at Yarmouth.

Jethro told me: "I still remember that night. I was told by Colin it was the Isle of Wight and not Cornwall and it was a much more sophisticated area. Would I keep the act clean? That meant only doing about five minutes instead of an hour. In the end I did the rude bits so fast the ladies thought I was singing."

In the early '90s Jethro sold out seven shows at Sandown Pavilion. It was fun just to see the expression on the faces of the more mature ladies in the audience. They had seen his spotless humour on Des O'Connor's shows and expected something similar. Those Denzil Penberthy stories were suddenly a little more illuminating than on television – and they loved it. They probably learnt a few new words, too.

At one of the shows I was happy to stand at the back. Suddenly a familiar face joined me – and I was caught in two minds. David Icke, who'd been a guest on my radio show a couple of years before Jethro, had recently come out as the Son of God. Should I laugh in such company? The 'Almighty' couldn't stop laughing – and neither could I.

On another occasion, when Jethro was making a weekly appearance at Sandown, I went down to try and get an interview but he was not in the mood and I quickly sensed this and went next door to interview his support act, my old friend and multi- *Opportunity Knocks* winner Berni Flint. As I left his dressing room Jethro shouted for me to go back into his room and said: "John come down next week and I'll do an interview for you."

Jethro did few interviews in subsequent years but I was always lucky. He once told me a local commercial radio presenter from East Anglia rang to interview him about a forthcoming local gig. The guy, amazingly, admitted he had no idea who Jethro was or what he did. The interview never took place.

I was so flattered in 2008 to be invited down to Jethro's home in Devon. He was the perfect host and we saw his famous club, had a tour of his stables and met some of the horses he'd bred. He even suggested a nearby pub where we could get a great evening meal, but also warned us not to go near a famous Cornish town that had acquired a somewhat tarnished reputation in recent years. We did cross the border later that day, when I did a second interview. This time it was with one of my favourite singers from the great Britpop days of the '90s, Louis Eliot from Rialto.

Back to Jethro. Just before leaving I asked him what he thought of the new breed of current British comedians. "Some of them are very good – if you don't want to laugh too much."

CHAPTER 76

Jimmy Tarbuck

SOME OF JIMMY TARBUCK'S celebrated showbiz friends were more than a little surprised in 1979 when he chose the Isle of Wight for his summer season, when the likes of Great Yarmouth and Blackpool would have welcomed him with open arms. On his return home in mid-September, from eight sold-out weeks at Sandown Pavilion, he had so much to tell them.

John Redgrave had persuaded Jimmy to come deep south and Tarby then tempted many of his pals to follow in his wake. Suddenly stars like Cilla Black, Bob Monkhouse, Norman Wisdom and Frankie Howerd summered at Sandown Pavilion.

It was such a personal thrill to finally meet JT. I will never forget his first-ever appearance on *Sunday Night At The London Palladium*, when he skipped on looking like the fifth Beatle. Well, he had gone to school with John Lennon. In those early days he came to Sandown for Sunday Concerts and there was never an empty seat. He used to run over time and one night he shouted to the show promoter, Don Moody, to throw on the keys and he would lock up. Within a few seconds, a huge set of keys flew in from the wings.

Such was his summer season success at Sandown Pavilion he returned in both 1981 and 1989. Holidaymakers had to move quickly for tickets as his local following was huge. The 1981 show is still fondly remembered as the greatest ever summer season show seen on the Isle of Wight. It was a stunning line-up with Kenny Lynch, Aiden J Harvey, Denise Nolan, Pans People and the Johnny Wiltshire Showband.

Through his scriptwriter, Wally Malston, I got to know Jimmy well in that '79 season and we have remained friends ever since. On a couple of occasions I have been up to the Coombe Hill Golf Club, where he's a member, to interview him and, quite rightly, they think the world of him. They have always gone out of their way to make me welcome.

I, like many others, was horrified by the way Jimmy was treated following the spate of much publicised arrests in the wake of Jimmy Savile and co.

He got a standing ovation when he was introduced by Bradley Walsh on *Live From The Palladium*. It was such an emotional return for him and millions of his fans.

He told me in 2015: "When you have problems with these ridiculous accusations, my god you find out who your friends are. Friends from the past in Australia and America even sent me letters. It was very touching that people took the time out to write to me and the family.

"I think the anonymous laws should be changed and these people who make the accusations should be named and let them come forward. I'm not sure what these liars are after. Is it five minutes of fame they want or are they trying to make money? I feel for all of those who were wrongly accused and then told everything had been dropped. I just thank the British public for sticking with Tarby."

For our 25th wedding anniversary, in 1988, Heather and myself were invited to spend a day at Jimmy's *Live From The London Palladium* Sunday night television show. We travelled up with Wally Malston, the script associate, and went for a walk near Jimmy's home while they worked on some of the gags for the show. Later in the day we spent a few minutes in Jimmy's dressing room. Some of the stars on that brilliant show were Tom Jones, Marti Caine, Sinitta, whose very short skirt created a few on stage cracks for Jimmy, Mark Walker, Eddy Grant and the Art Of Noise.

CHAPTER 77

Max Bygraves

I WAS LUCKY TO CATCH Max Bygraves' first ever appearance on the Isle of Wight. He had been once before but only for a private visit to Cowes on Billy Cotton's boat. He could see the white cliffs from his home in Bournemouth and didn't know it was so easy to get to.

When I was a kid Max was such a huge star and his brand of humour was a breath of fresh air and so different to many of the older comics who had been established for years. His catchphrases like "big 'ead", "I've arrived and to prove it I'm here" and "a good idea son" were the talk of the playground, as was *Educating Archie*, the radio show that gave Max his first real break. It's hard to believe now that others like Peter Sellers, Julie Andrews and Dick Emery also had a lot to thank Peter Brough for.

Max was such big box-office success and he quickly also became a movie star and appeared in hits like *A Cry From The Streets*, *Spare The Rod* and *Charlie Moon*. He did reveal that one of his greatest regrets featured a movie – and explained why.

"It was such a great accolade for me when Alfred Hitchcock, one of the world's greatest movie directors, actually wanted me for his film *Frenzy*. He had seen me in *A Cry From The Streets* and made me the offer.

"Unfortunately, I was under contract for a Manchester cabaret season and thousands of tickets had been sold and I couldn't get out of it."

He'd been christened Walter and his name change came about when he was in the RAF. On his very first night the new recruits were asked if any of them could perform. He'd been watching live variety shows at the New Cross Empire since he was a schoolboy and could do a few impressions. When he did Max Miller it brought the house down and he instantly became Max to his pals – and so it stayed.

When Max supported Judy Garland in a London Palladium show their four-week season was extended to 20. She was so impressed with his performances and invited him back to New York.

It always made me feel a little sad that a few later generations only knew Max from his days as the host of TV's *Family Fortunes* and his "big money" catchphrase. For others, it was probably just for his sing-a-long-a-Max albums. They knew nothing about our childhood favourites like *You're A Pink Toothbrush* and *Gilly Gilly Ossenfeffer*.

In his later years there were times when a few people, including the press, had a pop at Max. He was, however, so clever. Right through his life he knew what the public wanted and gave it to them. He had 31 gold discs to prove it.

The last time I saw Max perform it was a night to remember. He'd flown by helicopter to Warner's, Norton Grange, Yarmouth, and when he came on stage the whole audience just stood and applauded, before he'd done anything. Now that's a star for you.

I was also completely shocked when he actually told me he listened to my radio show, which could be heard all along the south coast. I was so flattered. I'd first listened to him when I was in a tin bath in front of the fire.

CHAPTER 78

Norman Wisdom

I ADMIT TO TWO ERRORS OF JUDGEMENT with respect to stars of British light entertainment. I had the opportunities to interview Dickie Henderson in 1980 and Norman Wisdom in 1982, both of whom were in long summer seasons right on my own doorstep. I know I would have been lucky on both occasions, if I had made the necessary requests. I put it down to a certain naivety in my early days as a showbiz writer. Regretfully, Dickie Henderson was the one I allowed to get away. I had a second chance with Norman and took it instantly.

That initial meeting, which was to prove the first of several over the next few years, finally came in 1990. At that time Norman was excited by the possibility of making a new film. Obviously we talked about all his movies that became worldwide hits. His Isle of Man neighbour, Rick Wakeman, was also imminent to making a new album with him. This subsequently came out and included some of Norman's own songs.

My next meeting with Sir Norman came in 1992 when I invited him to appear live on my Sunday lunchtime Isle of Wight Radio chat show. It was to prove a day I will never forget.

I picked Norman up from his hotel, near the theatre he was appearing at, and drove him to the radio station. He instantly volunteered to read the weather forecast and I feared the worst, as he was in a devilish mood. As anticipated, he carried on long after the weather bed jingle had finished. It was our longest ever and included sun, rain, thunder, snow and everything else possible from the sky.

Directly after the show I had to take him to a special event at the Frank James Hospital, in East Cowes, the town where I was born. Norman had been mobbed all over the world but on this occasion he got rather scared with so many people around him and asked me to take him inside to escape the crowds. Then came one of the most emotional moments of my life.

At that time our local hospice was being modernised and a mixed ward was temporarily set up at the Frank James Hospital. Norman was asked if he would visit the ward and he willingly agreed. As he entered the room he instantly switched on the real Norman Wisdom persona and became the funny man we'd all loved in those movies. He jumped on the beds, kissed all the ladies and shook hands with the men and did an act for about ten minutes. I was brought to tears as he entertained people who were clearly unwell. They loved every minute. Ironically, it brought back memories of a fantastic television play in which Norman had excelled as a man dying of cancer.

Then he was all set to visit two of his closest showbiz friends, comedy duo Billy Whittaker and Mimi Law, who lived about eight miles away. Billy, a superb pantomime dame, had worked with Norman on numerous occasions. He gave me my instructions – no main roads please, just country lanes. I managed that and we all had afternoon tea. Then Norman had a show to do in the evening.

A few years later we met up again in an Southampton hotel. I'd been invited by his PR lady to have lunch with them and then do a radio interview with him. During the meal she told me the room was all set up for our interview. Norman, who by then was slightly forgetful, asked what that was all about and added: "I wondered why John was having lunch with us." It went like a dream and he revealed the emotional story of how he and a pal had walked from London to Cardiff in search of work.

CHAPTER 79

Jane McDonald

WHEN *THE CRUISE* television series came on screen in 1998, I was so impressed with Jane McDonald and I was certainly not alone. Millions watched her progress in a tough environment and it eventually launched her glittering career. Jane's then new husband, Henrik Brixen, took over controlling her career and my interview requests were obviously cast aside. I must say, I never took to him at all in the television series.

Then the great PR lady Judy Totton came to my rescue. She was promoting a new Jane McDonald album and I had an invite to go to London's Berkeley Square. I sat underneath the trees but never even heard a nightingale. I did meet one a few minutes later but, on this occasion, she was not singing, just chatting. Jane is a person you warm to instantly and she lights up a room the minute you walk in. I have been privileged to have met her on several occasions. I'll never forget October 2006, when I interviewed her at the Congress Theatre, Eastbourne.

An interview had been set up for London but I had to cancel it because my wife was very ill in hospital. Sadly, Heather, who really was the wind beneath my wings, passed away. Jane was told about this and kindly offered to see me on tour. I arrived in Eastbourne, which was a favourite place for Heather and I, and felt really low. I even had to come out of a shop where we used to go in together.

A few minutes later I arrived at the Congress Theatre and was shown into a very comfortable room and told to wait for Jane. She walked in and said: "I've been thinking about you. Come here, I want to give you a big hug." That was just what I needed and I will always be grateful to her for that and the subsequent interview that got me working again.

Two years later I caught up with Jane again in London and we had great fun. She was promoting a superb double package of a CD and DVD, called Jane. She told me that title took a long time to think up.

I told her that while watching the DVD of her concert, it took my mind back to when she used to play an accordion on her chest. We'd talked about that in our first-ever interview.

"I was in the Wakefield Accordion Band and was rather good until I grew a bust and the accordion always seemed to get caught up in my jumper. That's why I switched to piano."

To my mind Jane is a 21st century Dorothy Squires. She's working class, very gutsy, a supreme entertainer with a powerful voice and gives it her all. Unbeknown to me, she'd been a fan of Dorothy Squires and was very flattered by my comparison.

Watching Jane in concert is an amazing experience and everyone has such fun, on and off stage. At that time 150,000 people had seen her on tour. She added: "The show's brilliant without me in it."

At that time it was 10 years after her television emergence on *The Cruise*. How did she manage to look younger than she did in the original show? Jane had an answer

"It was 10 years ago and you are 10 years older. I reckon your eyes are going."

She did admit she can't watch the original series anymore.

I had to ask her how the male guests felt when facing the girls on Loose Women.

"When they come on their body language is hilarious. They either cross their arms or cover their bits up. What are they expecting us to do – attack them?"

CHAPTER 80

Jim Davidson

JIM DAVIDSON WAS the red-hot favourite to win New Faces in 1976 and millions of us were surprised when he was beaten by a bear. I think Jim might have had a special name for it! Clive Green from Ryde's Ponda Rosa roadhouse came out of it very well. He'd booked young Jim as an unknown comic for a Saturday night dinner dance cabaret, for virtually next to nothing. Before that gig, due for early October, he'd been a national sensation on New Faces. Those were the good old days and Jim and his management honoured that booking.

It's hard to believe now but Jim was a very nervous young man in those days, with frequent dry mouth problems and was even rather worried about performing for 200 diners. We did a pre-show interview and I tried to calm him down and build up his confidence. Suddenly he was on stage and in brilliant form. He was doing his early "nick nick" police routine and there was not a rude joke in sight.

Always looking for a photo opportunity to go with my showbiz articles for the Isle of Wight Weekly Post, I rang up the most notorious copper around and asked him if he could come in a picture with Jim and pretend to be arresting him. David Gurd, a feared speed cop, was certainly up for it. Then the chief of police heard about it and would not give his permission. Jim did raise a glass to the local police, as pictured.

Following New Faces, Jim had been quickly booked for other TV shows like Seaside Special, Celebrity Sweepstakes and What's On Next?

Jim counted himself lucky to have had his chance via a hit television series and modestly had a word for those who had not been so fortunate. He told me: "There are so many good comics about not on TV. I am working here tonight and the place is packed because I've been on television. There might be unknown comics three times as good as me but they suffer because no one has heard of them and so the punters don't turn out to see them."

I have known Jim for over 40 years and interviewed him on several occasions. He's only really disappointed me once but he's more than compensated for that since then. After my wife died he willingly agreed to talk to me to help focus my mind back on work and I'm always grateful for that and to a mutual friend who made it possible.

Over the years, I have loved his major pantomimes and his great comedy routines with the late Roger Kitter, who had so much talent. I won't mention Sinderella.

I actually met Jim exactly 40 years after that initial Ponda Rosa gig. He came back to the Isle of Wight and gave me a very honest and emotional interview. He was another showbiz star who was falsely accused in the Operation Yewtree investigation. He revealed the stress problems it caused. The audience, who were clearly on his side, roared their approval and gave him a standing ovation. I can't say there weren't any rude jokes on that occasion. There was an annoying lady heckler and he dealt with her superbly. The hallmark of a real professional.

CHAPTER 81

Shaw Taylor

IN OVER 40 YEARS OF INTERVIEWING famous people, I've got to know many for just the duration of our interview, others have become friends and a few close pals. Shaw Taylor certainly fell into the latter category. During the last 18 years of his life, he lived in Totland Bay, on the Isle of Wight, and proved a very respected resident. Over the years we became such close friends, as did our respective partners.

Shaw, such a likeable and generous man, was one of the most famous faces in Great Britain for many years – despite his *Police 5* show being just five minutes. It was scheduled for six weeks and ran for 30 years. He did appear in so many other programmes and was a supreme professional. He had the skill of looking as if he knew a lot about a certain subject, when, in some cases, he didn't.

He once told me: "I don't think 'Hurricane' Higgins was too impressed with my snooker knowledge. There were rumours of just where he wanted to stick his cue – and it would have been painful."

There were stories I got him to repeat as often as possible, as I just never tired of hearing them. Before he became a television legend Shaw was a West End actor and had appeared in the original London production of *The Hollow*. They asked him if he would like to appear in their next thriller, called *The Mousetrap*. He declined and said it wouldn't last and 50 years later he was still laughing about his error of judgement. In reality, he made the right decision. He surprised his fellow thespian pals by going into television. They thought he was mad – until they found out what he was earning.

Only Shaw Taylor could have got away with an impromptu live television interview with Khrushchev at a British Trade Fair in Moscow. When he was at Radio Luxembourg he became the first DJ to interview the Beatles.

He was also often mistaken for Peter Sellers – and it was vice versa. Sellers once asked Shaw what he did if people thought it was him.

"I told him that if movies were mentioned, I signed as Peter Sellers but if *Police 5* was mentioned I signed as Shaw Taylor. When Peter was mistaken for me he told them he was, and then to '**** off.' A pal of mine once jumped into Peter's car at traffic lights in London, thinking it was me. Apparently Peter was not too amused."

Shaw and his partner, Shirley, often took me and my new partner, Bertie, out for meals at the wonderful George Hotel in Yarmouth. On one occasion a group of well behaved yuppies were sat not far from us. As they went, one of them came over to personally thank Shaw for all his great work on television in past years. Shaw thanked him and I sensed just how touched he was by the comment.

Sadly, I saw Shaw at home the day before he died. He was very poorly, but I managed to make him smile with my very bad impression of "keep 'em peeled" his famous catchphrase.

Shaw had such a wicked sense of humour and would have loved his final exit. As the undertakers were trying to carry him downstairs, avoiding the tricky stair lift, the house lights all went out, due to a power cut. His partner's sister was heard to comment: "Trust Shaw to go out with a bang!"

I was privileged to attend his Memorial Service at the Covent Garden Actors Church. Many came to celebrate his life and some great stories were related. They even showed the moment Noel Edmunds caught him out with a Gotcha.

CHAPTER 82

Vince Hill

I FIRST BECAME A FAN of Vince Hill back in the '60s when he sang live every Wednesday lunchtime on the Light Programme's *Parade Of The Pops*. It was compulsive listening, with Denny Piercy hosting the show and Vince out-singing some of the original artists, on his versions of their hit songs, backed by Bob Miller and the Millermen. I still have his original singles on Pye Piccadilly and his debut album, *Have you Met ...?* on Columbia.

It was my copies of his early EMI albums that first led me to meeting Vince. It was around 1973 when he did several concerts at Sandown Pavilion. Being great fans, my wife Heather and myself made a point of meeting him after the show and getting our records signed. On one was a picture of Vince and his new baby boy, Athol. We knew

Vince and his wife Annie had waited a long time for Athol and during our friendly chat we confessed we had been trying for 11 years.

He was a great comfort and inspiration to us and said: "Never give up. We waited at least 13 years and it will happen." He was proved so right. Sean was born in 1974.

Many years later I met Athol at Vince's home and told him the story of how his birth had given us such real hope. Sadly, he died in 2014, following the after-effects of a road traffic accident. That news was so hard to take.

Two years after meeting Vince for the first time, as a pure fan, I began writing a showbiz column for the *Isle Of Wight Weekly Post*, which, thankfully, really took off and I interviewed him in 1981. The venue was Sandown Pavilion but this time it was on a professional basis. We really hit it off and became friends. So much so that for many years when Vince came for his regular Isle of Wight gigs, in theatres and holiday centres, I was his volunteer driver and picked him and his musical director up from the ferry to take them to gigs and then their late night return.

Over the years I continued to buy Vince's albums, enjoyed his hit television series like *They Sold A Million*, the radio play about the Tolpuddle Martyrs, for which he wrote the music with the brilliant Ernie Dunstall, and his superb *My Dearest Ivor* musical play, in memory of Ivor Novello.

A long term ambition of mine was to do an 'at home' interview with Vince at his house on the banks of the River Thames. In 2012 this all came to fruition when Bertie and I were invited to his gorgeous home at Shipley. Sat in the room above his boathouse, Vince was in wonderful form and we recorded an hours conversation, which made a two-hour radio special,

Just after the interview I actually felt very important for a few moments. Vince went to help Annie get the lunch and I was left on my own just a few yards from the Thames. When the boats passed and their occupants waved, I waved back, hoping they would think all this was mine.

Sadly, in 2016 Vince lost his lovely wife Annie. He had also enjoyed the company of my late wife, Heather, who gave me such great support.

My two favourite Vince Hill tracks are *Unexpectedly* and *Come What May*. The first was a single, which should have made the charts, and the other a Eurovision-winning song of which his version even tops the original.

CHAPTER 83

Paul Daniels & Debbie McGee

WHEN I WENT TO THE HOME of Vince Hill, we talked about some of his friends who also lived on the banks of the River Thames in Berkshire. I had interviewed both Paul Daniels and Debbie McGee in past years and suggested how I would love to do an 'at home' with them. Vince said he would put the idea to them and see how they felt. In less than three months, Bertie and I were heading for their wonderful home. We were early and I phoned just to say we'd arrived in the area. Debbie told me they were just having lunch and had saved some for us. So we quickly joined them.

I'd always got on well with Paul and Debbie but had never interviewed them together. The very first time I met Paul was at a Warner's holiday centre on Hayling Island. Sean, who was studying to become a journalist, came with me. I'll never forget my first view of Paul. He welcomed us and was sat in a chair with his arms firmly folded. It seemed he was going to make me work to get the best out of him. I was up for the challenge and had managed to overcome my first test. It went well and I got used to his kind of off-beat sense of humour.

When I took down my recording equipment, I noticed his microphone was switched off. I could feel a certain panic coming on, but remained calm. We departed and on our way back to the car, I revealed my fears to Sean. I was recording on a DAT machine in those days and quickly tried the interview and all was well. I think that Paul had discreetly turned the switch off to give me a fright.

The next time we met was when I'd arranged to see Debbie for an interview and I think he was pleased – and he disappeared very quickly. I did meet him a year or two later at a golf club, where he was arranging a special tournament.

The last time I saw Paul was when I recorded that special programme at their home in 2011. They were such perfect hosts. He showed us his magic room where many of the tricks were made, stored and perfected. It was a fascinating look into the life of a superstar magician. We had the grand tour and there was time for a few photographs. Selfies had not been invented and we used a real camera.

The hour-long interview was even better than I imagined and they were such a great double act and the instinctive repartee between them added so much to the success of the programme. A few years earlier, Paul had recorded a great voicer to advertise my radio programme. It went something like this: "You are listening to *John Hannam Meets* on Isle of Wight Radio. You'll like it – not a lot – but you'll like it." This time Debbie did one, with a real sexy voice. I'm not going to reveal that one.

Following her appearance on Mrs Merton's television show there were frequent press quotes about the question she was asked. I never found it funny at the time or afterwards. On that day by the River Thames, I realised just why she had married Paul Daniels. It had nothing to do with money – she just fell in love with him. It was still so obvious how they felt about each other and this remained until his untimely death in 2016.

CHAPTER 84

Lynn Farleigh & John Woodvine

THEY JUST HAPPEN TO BE two of my favourite actors and, rather conveniently, they are a married couple. In 2004, they were both in a play at the Nuffield Theatre, Southampton, and I interviewed Lynn. At the end of her interview, which was so enjoyable, I asked if she might put in a good word for me with John, who didn't undertake that many interviews. Within a few days, I was back at the Nuffield, with one of the most famous movie doctors of all time. John played Dr Hirsch in *An American Werewolf In London*, a real cult movie. Little did I realise that these two separate interviews would lead to a personal friendship.

Two years later they were booked for a short season at the Chichester Festival Theatre. They had agreed to be interviewed together. Sadly, a family tragedy meant I had to call off the arranged interview – and they were so sympathetic. A few weeks later, when it was really too late to plug their show, they still welcomed me to Chichester and I appreciated their gesture. From that occasion we regularly kept in touch.

A few years later I was in Birmingham at the home of brilliant musician Bev Bevan and realised they lived not too far away and quite close to our route south. I rang John and he said Lynn was working but would we still like to pop in for tea. I set the satnav and ended up in a Ministry of Defence property. The guard at the gate was not too surprised, it had happened before. We were well and truly lost and in the end, I phoned John on my mobile and he guided us in. In the meantime, he had nipped out for a lovely cake and we had a tea party in their delightful garden.

Back on the Isle of Wight, I ran the local *County Press Theatre Awards* and invited them down as surprise guests – and they readily agreed. It worked like a dream. Lynn appeared on stage in the first half and, in between the presentations, we talked about her career, with stories about playing Wycliffe's long-suffering wife in the hit TV series and her memorable appearance in the waterbed episode of *Steptoe And Son*. After her first appearance in the second half, I talked about her famous husband and suggested that if he walked on stage now it would bring the house down – and it did. It was a complete surprise and John had been on television hundreds of times.

The next day we took them on a tour of the Isle of Wight and Lynn was keen to find the shop her father once owned. I became excited, as I knew where it was. In my earlier life, I'd worked as a salesman for United Biscuits. I took her straight to Farleigh's Stores in Ventnor.

John with Lynn Farleigh and John Woodvine

Sean and his future wife Susie, unexpectedly, led me back to John and Lynn. We were visiting her parents for the first time and they were not too far from the Woodvines. I had rung Lynn to ask if there was an hotel nearby. "Don't be so silly, you're going to stay with us," she insisted. They were the perfect hosts.

I did have a shock the next day when we arrived back home. I had put my jacket on their newel post, over John's. When I picked it up the next day, I took his as well, but didn't discover it until we were on the ferry. I posted it back the same night. Whoops!

CHAPTER 85

Ken Stott

OVER THE YEARS IN WEST SUSSEX I've interviewed so many amazing actors, including some of my own personal favourites. The PR ladies at the Chichester Festival Theatre have been so good to me and in early 2017 Lucinda Morrison went out of her way to obtain me a much sought-after interview with Ken Stott. I always eagerly await their press releases and set up my targets – and most times they come off.

Ken Stott had arrived in Chichester direct from a West End run in Ronald Harwood's classic play *The Dresser*. We arrived in the city and were walking from the station when Ken passed us, but I resisted any temptation to talk to him. I always remember sitting in a Chichester cafe near another great actor, Roy Dotrice, but I never interrupted his lunch to say I was interviewing him later. I did tell him later he'd been spotted, but I know he was grateful to have been left alone.

Sadly, Ken was not out walking around this beautiful Sussex city. It turned out he was very unwell and had been heading for the pharmacy. In fact, after each show, he went to bed to try and aid his recovery from an actors' curse, a really heavy cold. When he arrived for the interview, which I imagine was the last thing he really needed, he went out of his way to welcome us. Bertie, who works in a pharmacy, was able to advise him with regard to the medicines he had purchased. Being a fan of Ken's portrayal of Rebus, she was more than happy to help.

For me, Ken has always been one of those actors that if I see he's in a particular television series or movie, I watch it. As yet, I've never been disappointed. He's got real charisma – on and off screen. Even when he's got a heavy cold.

I was surprised to find that Ken was a singer before he became an actor. In Scotland he had worked with a couple of musicians who went on to play with the Bay City Rollers. After leaving drama school he was thrilled to play in Still Life, a progressive rock band. Then an acting chance came in Ireland and he was away.

Ken was full of fun and stories. After working for the Royal Shakespeare Company, he ran into debt and became a double glazing salesman to make some money. He called on a huge house where two sisters lived and his problem was solved.

"You are told to quote a price and then say nothing, which I did. One said to the other 'so, it's the windows or the holiday.' I was thinking take the holiday, but they had the windows."

Amazingly, a few years later he actually played a double glazing salesman in *Taking Over The Asylum*.

During his career Ken was such a hit in series like *The Vice*, *Rebus*, where he was so much more suited to the part than John Hannah, and *Messiah*.

"We were particularly proud of The *Vice*, where we treated the prostitutes as actually being the victims. A taxi driver once told me it had changed his thinking and that he now had a different view about street girls.

"*Messiah* was altogether different and was violence for violence sake," said Ken.

I think he was superb in *Rebus*, who had rather a troubled personal life. I found it so amusing that as Rebus he was a Hibernian supporter when, in real life, his passion is for Hearts, their bitter rivals.

Ken also revealed how thrilled he was to be in the original West End production of *Art*, with Tom Courtenay and Albert Finney. Some nights it was almost with disbelief that he realised just who he was on stage with.

CHAPTER 86

Les Dennis

UNLIKE SOME OTHER JOURNALISTS, I have never been interested in the private life of Les Dennis – and he has appreciated this. Over the years, he has always been such a pleasure to talk to. The press coverage given to one of his former wives bored me to tears years ago. To my mind, he is far more talented than he is ever credited for. My belief in him was even more justified when I saw him brilliantly perform that huge speech in *Art*. No wonder the audience just roared their approval.

Les came in the tried and trusted route of '70s light entertainment stars – the impressionist shows. He was one of the first, other than Mike Yarwood and Peter Goodwright. Soon to follow him were newcomers like Bobby Davro, Gary Wilmot and Mike Osman and co. Many still remember the great comedy partnership he had with the late Dustin Gee. They had met on the Russ Abbot Show and were an instant hit. Their Vera and Mavis routine from *Coronation Street* won them millions of fans and their own Laughter Show on television.

Back in 1986, the first time we ever met, Les reflected on those days.

"All at once I had to get used to being in a double act and dressing up as a woman, something I had never imagined.

"When Dustin tragically died, he left me with a stepping stone. I am better now as a solo act than I was in the early days of my career. In a way it's a lot easier now to go out on my own, as people know what to expect from me."

Hosting *Family Fortunes* for 15 years also introduced Les to a whole new audience and he took this show high into the TV ratings charts. The *Les Dennis Laughter Show* was also a huge hit on television.

During our first-ever interview Les hinted of a change of direction. At that time his ideal night off was, surprisingly, not to go to a pantomime or light entertainment show. Often he headed to Stratford or the National to watch superb actors in top-quality productions.

Liverpool has always been a hotbed for comedians and singers but Les was keen to break into serious acting and in recent years has been acclaimed for so many outstanding performances. Who could have guessed, when he was so famous for his Mavis take off, that he would eventually turn up as the character Michael Rodwell in *Coronation Street*? It was a long way from almost getting the first-ever maximum points on *New Faces*.

Les certainly proved his critics wrong. There was Amos Hart in *Chicago*, seasons in *Hairspray*, *Legally Blonde* and *Spamalot* and a movie with Julie Walters.

I can remember a memorable day at the Orchard Theatre, Dartford, when I interviewed

the three stars of a national tour of *Art*, after an afternoon matinee. What an occasion that was, with Les, John Duttine and Christopher Cazenove. They were a great team both on and off stage. What a great shock when Christopher died in 2010.

Back in 1990, Les played a summer season at the Sandown Pavilion. His previous visits were all for one-nighters. It finally gave him a chance to explore. He stayed in the picturesque village of Wroxall and I ran into him one day with his shopping basket in the local Spar store.

When he was rehearsing for the six-week show he left the theatre at around 8.15 on a Saturday night to appear live on my radio show. They all stopped and listened to the show. When he got back to rehearsals they gave him a round of applause – and it was much deserved. That was for him – not me!

And finally...
Coronation Street

MY GOOD FRIEND Vic Farrow, a former local cinema owner, show promoter and Shanklin Theatre booker, has been so helpful to me in recent years and he managed to obtain me a much cherished 1995 interview with Sir Cliff Richard, which is included in my 2016 book, featuring my stories behind interviewing the pop stars of the '50s, '60s and '70s.

In August 2001, thanks to Vic and his friend Peter Shaw, a first assistant director on Coronation Street, I was invited up to Manchester to visit the set and interview some of the stars of the soap. I spoke to Peter the day before and he asked if I was happy with the two cast members the press office had arranged for me. I think he quickly sensed I was not impressed with the two lesser-known characters chosen. He told me not to worry and that we could see how the day progressed.

Being a true Islander, I wanted to get up and back in the same day. I caught the 4am ferry from East Cowes to Southampton and then walked to the station to get a train to Oxford. This was around 5.30. At Oxford I caught a train to Manchester. I was scheduled to arrive in the city at 10.20am. As I left the train, a miracle happened – it was exactly 10.20.

When I arrived at the studios there were actors busily learning their lines. Peter put me in the children's play room, as there were none on set that day, and I set up my equipment. I had done my research on my two actors and did a few more, just in case. After the two arranged interviews were recorded, the two PR girls left and Peter told me to sit tight. Apparently, there was talk outside of the room that the guy doing the interviews would let each guest choose a record. All of a sudden in quick succession came Sean Wilson (Martin Platt), Bruce Jones (Les Battersby), Jimmy Harkishin (Dev Alahan), Helen Worth (Gail Platt), Bill Tarmey (Jack Duckworth) and Liz Dawn (Vera Duckworth). I could scarcely believe it.

From that visit I was invited by Liz Dawn to her Breast Cancer Charity Gala Show at Leeds, a few weeks later, where I got another dozen interviews.

By the way, I did get back home on the same day from that visit to the studio. It was a 20-hour round trip.

John with Liz Dawn

Snorbitz and Bernie Winters with John